This Book is
Protected by
Instant IP

Advanced Praise for
The Code to Collaboration

"Very few people can see connections others miss—and even fewer can explain how to act on them. Chad Jenkins does both. This book captures his decades of pattern recognition and turns it into a repeatable system you can use to create value through collaboration."

— Shannon Waller
Author of the *Team Success Handbook*, *Multiplication by Subtraction*, and co-author of *Superpowered*

"In a world less than fifty years into the 21st century, Chad Jenkins is helping us crack the code on what success looks like now. In the agrarian age, it was the guild. In the industrial age, it was the union. In the age of intellectual capitalism, it will be The Collaborative. Chad makes a compelling case that the future does not belong to collectivism on one extreme or cartels on the other, but to ambitious people who learn how to co-labor, co-create, and multiply value together. *The Code to Collaboration* is a must-read for entrepreneurs, their teams, their clients, and even their competitors who may one day become their greatest collaborators."

— Tony D'Angelo
Creator of The Intellectual Capitalist®

"Most books teach you how to do more. This book teaches you how to see differently. Chad Jenkins reveals that collaboration isn't a tactic—it's the original operating system for humanity. Once you read this, you'll never look at ideas, growth, or people the same way again."

— Dean Jackson
New Information, Inc., I Love Marketing

"I rarely write endorsements unless I've taken the time to truly understand the thinking behind the work. In Chad Jenkins' case, that understanding comes from years of conversation, observation, and seeing how he thinks—not just what he teaches.

"We are living in a world that rewards speed, noise, and competition,yet quietly starves people of meaning, trust, and alignment. *The Code to Collaboration* speaks directly to that gap. Chad reminds us that collaboration is not a tactic for growth—it is a way of being that honors how people were designed to create, contribute, and multiply impact together.

"What I appreciate most about this book is that it doesn't ask people to become someone else. It helps them recognize what they already carry, and then shows how combining those gifts—intentionally and generously—creates outcomes no individual effort can sustain. In a time when so many are chasing success in isolation, this book offers a wiser, more human path forward."

— Lee Brower
Founder, Empowered Wealth™

"Chad Jenkins is an alchemist. His catalyst to create massive new opportunity is collaboration, and once you've seen him do it, you can't unsee it.

"I've sat across from Chad and watched him listen to an entrepreneur describe their business. Five minutes in, he's already connecting dots nobody else can see. He doesn't brainstorm. He doesn't workshop. Something fires in his brain, and he sees the whole field: your past, your present, your future, and every combination in between. He calls it Dimensional Vision Awareness. I call it his superpower. And then, he gives you the combination that changes your trajectory.

"The thing about Chad is he didn't keep this gift to himself. He reverse-engineered it. He built the VCR Formula, the Declaration of Collaboration, the I AM Process, and a community called CoLAB, where entrepreneurs show up with what they've been given and split the outcome. More than 700 collaborations have come out of that community, and the rate is accelerating.

"Here's why that matters right now. The attention economy, the one that rewarded whoever could capture the most eyeballs and hoard the most information, is running out of road. AI is collapsing execution time so fast that the bottleneck is no longer getting things done. The bottleneck is finding the right person to combine with.

"We're entering the collaboration economy, and Chad has been building its operating system for years. Every entrepreneur I know wakes up with more ideas than they can act on. As our mentor, Dan Sullivan, taught us in *Who Not How*®, they're missing the who, not the how.
Chad built CoLAB because he could see that gap before the rest of us could name it. This book gives you the code he's been using all along.

"Read it. Then go build your first collaboration. The future belongs to the people who collaborate."

— Steve French

Founder, infomatix; Co-Founder, AI Simplifier; CoLAB Architect

The Code to Collaboration

How to Collect and Combine to Create
the Future You Were Designed to Live

Other Books By Chad T. Jenkins

Just Add a Zero
Friction Fuel
The VCR Formula (co-authored with Dean Jackson)

More Books from CoVerse Collective

SEEDSPARK.com/CoVerse

The Code to Collaboration

How to Collect and Combine to Create the Future You Were Designed to Live

Chad T. Jenkins

To humanity—
May we remember that giving is our nature,
collaboration is our design,
and together we can create
what none of us could alone.

Contents

Foreword

Chad Jenkins has a rare ability to look at already successful entrepreneurs and reveal a far bigger game hiding in plain sight. He starts from a bold premise: you're not missing anything essential. Your next level of creativity, productivity, and profitability won't come from fixing weaknesses, but from compounding your existing strengths through **Collaboration Currency**—plugging your reliability, courage, and drive into the right people, structures, and opportunities for exponential impact and enjoyment.

Chad has a way of listening for five minutes and seeing more of you than you've seen of yourself in five years. In my 52 years of coaching entrepreneurs, he is one of the deepest thinkers I've met, with x-ray vision for how you can multiply the impact and value of capabilities you already have. When this collaborator looks at an entrepreneur, he doesn't see gaps; he sees underused assets waiting to be compounded.

Collaboration Currency starts from a radical premise: you're not missing anything essential. The real constraint isn't what you lack—it's that you're trying to use what you already have in isolation. Your strengths are fine; it's the way you organize and deploy them that needs an upgrade.

As a strategic thinking partner, Chad shows you that you're already built for serious impact. You bring practical judgment, follow-through, and the ability to turn ideas into results, plus more initiative and courage than you realize. He treats these as strategic capabilities that can be aimed and combined.

When he reflects them back, you stop seeing quirks and start seeing a powerful toolkit that has been there all along, waiting to be used at a much higher level.

From this vantage point, **Collaboration Currency** is both simple and transformative:

Your strengths become exponentially more valuable when plugged into the right people and structures that support them.

Your persistence becomes a platform others can stand on.

Your bias for action becomes the spark that gets everyone moving and keeps important projects from stalling out.

Chad dismantles the myth that you must "fix yourself" before collaborating. Your individuality, self-reliance, and even stubbornness are treated as premium assets. Properly channeled, they give any collaboration clarity, direction, and staying power. Instead of softening who you are, this approach sharpens it and plugs it into the right partnerships, so you feel more like yourself as you grow, not less.

Collaboration Currency is compounding, not linear. Your reliability creates trust; your courage prevents stall; your drive attracts builders and long-term partners. Chad teaches you to connect these pieces so your future stops being a solo project and becomes a co-created multiplying engine, where your best capabilities—and theirs— continually make each other bigger in ways you couldn't engineer alone.

If you're a seasoned entrepreneur, this is your invitation to retire the solo-hero script and step into a much larger arena. Chad Jenkins will show you how to re-organize your existing capabilities into a trusted platform that attracts top collaborators and bigger opportunities.

As you apply Collaboration Currency, your creativity sharpens, your productivity accelerates, and your profitability compounds—turning the next chapter of your entrepreneurial life into your most enjoyable and impactful yet.

— Dan Sullivan, Co-Founder of Strategic Coach®

Part One: Identify

Chapter One

Designed for Collaboration

I constantly hear people say they saw a new product or service introduced in a commercial or ad on social media, only to realize they had the same idea three years earlier. It's frustrating to realize you missed the opportunity to monetize your concept and present it to the world. But it makes you wonder what the difference is between you and the person making money on your fantastic idea.

I guarantee that someone reading this book woke up with a better idea this morning. Maybe it was you. You dealt with some friction—a problem or grievance—yesterday, and while you were sleeping, you figured out a way to make the job easier. You saw a better way to keep your tea filled when you are out to lunch, or you came up with a polite suggestion for someone working on your home. The general public doesn't lack ideas; we just don't know how to act on them.

Every idea for improvement has the potential to turn you into an entrepreneur or take your entrepreneurship to the next level. Today, we use the term entrepreneur to define a small business owner, but in the 1800s, Jean Baptiste Say coined the word, saying that an "entrepreneur shifts economic resources out of an area of lower and into an area of higher productivity and greater yield."[1]

You don't have to be the owner of the company to be an entrepreneur. Many give themselves this title; however, if you want to call yourself one, you need to relentlessly seek leverage. Whenever you have an idea to take existing resources currently performing at one level and increase their level, you are, by definition, an entrepreneur.

If you've ever acted on an idea to improve your life, you are an entrepreneur. Your level of entrepreneurship depends on whether you are willing to move forward with your ideas. The amount of time people spend being entrepreneurial seems directly tied to their awareness of how to take action. You already have everything you need, but how do you take your vision to the next level? How can you get your idea off the ground? My friend Dan Sullivan tells entrepreneurs that multiplier growth means you Make it Up, Make it Real, and Make it Recur^{TM}. Your vision is the make-it-up phase, but how do you make it real and make it recur? That's where the Code to Collaboration comes in.

From the Beginning

Collaboration is the ultimate leverage. It has the power to give you an uncommon advantage. In fact, all true entrepreneurs lead with a collaboration-first growth strategy. And while many people think the most lucrative entrepreneurs were born with a silver spoon, as I've studied successful leaders, I realize most started with nothing. With no trust fund to lean on, they had to learn how to leverage what they had from an early age, and they never forgot it.

Every pivotal moment in human history has its roots in entrepreneurs taking collaborative action. We find the fundamentals of collaboration in the building blocks of humanity. They trace all the way back to when humans didn't want to be someone else's lunch. Think about the size and speed of humans compared to the animals at the top of the food chain. How in the world did we survive? Early men and women brought their creativity together to keep the lions and tigers from eating them.

One man figured out striking flint on iron would allow them to harness fire, another had building skills, and a third had a vision for a fortification that would keep the wild animals away from their families. Someone else looked at the fire and the structure and thought, "What if the builder could put something over the fire?" "What if we heated meat and eggs over the fire?" Eventually, curiosity led them to grind wheat kernels with two stones, while a woman watched and envisioned a technique to combine wheat flour, water, eggs, and fire to make a delicious treat.

They let their imaginations and capabilities run wild to level up their creations. Cooking fires and stone structures became forging furnaces and kilns. Together, humans learned how to make sharp instruments and pottery. These collaborations inspired artisans to decorate their clay pots and combine gems with fine metal to create jewelry. Michelangelo took this to the next level, making specific hues by combining the pigments nature gave him to create a collaboration that drove the uniqueness of his paintings. Entrepreneurship, in the sense of making things better, and collaboration not only kept them alive; it made life more beautiful.

Where It Went Wrong

I believe every human on the planet was born to be an entrepreneur, according to Jean Baptiste Say's definition. Our parents were correct when they told us we are all made unique and have tremendous ideas and insights to share. There's one problem: no one told us what to do with our uniqueness. It's become my passion to remedy that.

On top of our lack of understanding how to use our own version of special, since the dawn of creation, humans also had to be on the lookout for other humans. Bad actors have always been part of the mix. It didn't take long for them to start managing one another, creating ideologies to keep the troublemakers in line. Of course, they needed some sort of code of behavior with penalties for breaking the rules. But regulations soon turned collaboration for the good of all into competition for the good of one.

Throughout history, when men, women, and even countries have worked together for mutual good, we have seen exponential outcomes, not just linear growth. However, when someone begins looking out for their own interests, chaos ensues. The Biblical account of Cain and Abel set the stage. Everything was going well until the older twin became jealous of his brother and killed him in the field.

We see the effects of competition in ancient history. Rome and Carthage worked well together until both wanted to control the trade routes. Athens led Greece in a union that protected the country and attracted immigrants until people with money and power decided they wanted to be in charge. Then the Athenians started to throw their weight around. Every time the collaboration moves into competition, the result is war.

For thousands of years, competition has caused people to miss out on the beauty of collaboration. Worse still, it kept them from reaching their full potential. Everything you see at this moment started in someone's imagination and came into being through collaboration, but we continue to train the next generation to hold themselves back. When humans busy themselves with comparisons and competition, they waste valuable time and resources. Comparisons and competition kill our entrepreneurial spirit and force us to settle for mediocrity.

Uniquely Created for Collaboration

Ironically, while most people don't understand true collaboration, it has been keeping you alive since before you were born. Your mom and dad collaborated to create something new and beautiful, namely, you! Inside the womb, you collaborated with your mother. She kept you alive, and your fetal cells traveled around in her blood and organs, boosting her immune system and sometimes targeting injury sites to help in healing.[2] You both just did what you do naturally—nothing more, nothing less—but it provided mutual benefit.

Within minutes of our births, a new collaboration began as caregivers—parents, guardians, and medical professionals—worked with us to help us grow and build lives we could enjoy. Unknowingly, these people who cared for us instilled the fundamentals of collaboration. They also shared a truth every responsible adult passes along to children.

From our youngest days, we're told we're unique. Mister Rogers instilled the truth in children for several generations, telling them, "You're special. There's no one just like you." But here's the friction: we were given this beautiful message, but no one told us how to activate it.

My purpose in life is to change that, to help every person on the planet return to the freedom of their childhood. The Code to Collaboration is the key to activating your uniqueness, embracing your one-of-a-kind ideas to combine what already exists to create new value, and releasing the competitive mindset that keeps you from being everything you were created to be. It is the roadmap to living the adventure of an Exponential Entrepreneur™, someone who never dismisses their ideas and imagination, creates value through their vision to help others, abandons comparisons and competition, and thrives in a space of combination and collaboration.

Every child should have the self-confidence that comes with knowing they are one of a kind. But generations of competition have stolen humanity's ability to understand what makes us unique or what we should do with our uniqueness. By the time they reach the third grade, kids start to compare themselves to others. Adolescents who fall short in the book-smart or athletic-smart categories of uniqueness stop believing this foundational principle.

Ever since humans created an organized education system, if one child got all the answers correct, every child expected they should be able to do the same. But when not every student understood math or picked it up as quickly as the child gifted in math, those who couldn't keep up felt bad. The same thing happened in English class and after school when kids gathered to play ball. Instead of recognizing our unique gifts, we compare and compete.

We were created for collaboration; however, society has wired us for competition. How might things change if each child embraced their uniqueness and combined their gifts? What would happen if the student gifted in math worked with the child who excelled in English until both got better in the areas they struggled with?

Collaboration isn't new. It spins all around us every moment. It's the root of everything we know. Your entire life and everything in it is a collaboration. Most often it's accidental. Without understanding this most profound, albeit simple code, collaborations just happen. But what if we could engineer these combinations to unlock massive leverage in all we do and all we are? Unlocking and embracing an awareness of collaborations allows us to reach our full potential and live the dreams we haven't begun to dream. It's the secret to all creation and the answer to taking those ideas you make up in the shower and making them "real" and then making them "recur." An awareness of collaborations will take you one step closer to exponential growth and a more beautiful life.

The First Key

The Code to Collaboration isn't complicated, but like any code, it seems mysterious to most. To decipher it, you need a key. The first key is attentiveness. Consider all the imagination it took to get this book into your hands. Someone observed the friction of writing on stone and pottery and imagined a better surface. Another person received the idea to take wood pulp and form it into paper. Inks were uncovered, presses invented, binding perfected, and books were born. Metals, fuel, batteries, and engines made delivery systems possible. But how many people think about all those collaborations when they find a package on their front porch?

Even before recorded history, humans worked together to produce a mutually beneficial outcome. Today, we take these basic collaborations for granted. Developing an awareness of the collaborations that surround you will take you one step closer to restoring your creator mindset.

Today, start making lists—preferably physical—of the collaborations that have happened over the last several thousand years just to make your life comfortable. And while you're at it, start paying more attention to the ideas you have every day. Don't let them go. Write down those visions that would fix a problem or make something better. Everyone has them, but most of us dismiss them. This newfound attentiveness will be your first key to cracking the Code to Collaboration, the gateway to seeing your ideas showcased in the next commercial.

Chapter Two

From Competition to Collaboration

The world seems to applaud the "go-getters" of each era. Some become famous, others end up on a pedestal, but most simply stand out in their community. Go-getters never stop. They wake up in the middle of the night with ideas and work all day to implement them.

Competition seems to be their ally because they want to get ahead of everyone else, and that drive appears to give them energy. But most of the competition-driven people I talk to start to get very tired by their fortieth birthday. Instead of living for their passion, they're living to win, and life becomes difficult.

The Go-Givers

I probably would have been labeled as a go-getter as a child. Curiosity sent me looking for the next problem I could solve. Imagination gave me ideas to reduce the friction, and a little implementation generally meant monetization.

But the more I learn about my innate passion to reduce friction and facilitate collaboration, the more I'm convinced it's not the go-getters who are the heroes; it's what Bob Burg calls the "go-givers."[3]

I've come to the conclusion that the only thing we can do in life is give what we've been given and split the outcome™. The Declaration of Independence says we've been endowed by our Creator with certain unalienable rights. But we've also been endowed with ideas and talents, unique Vision, Capabilities, and Reach. To the extent you subscribe to the "give what you have been given" and "split the outcome" lifestyle, you will also begin to live a life you have only dreamt of.

My curiosity and imagination have been given to me. My ability to see how two things can come together and create something new and beneficial has been gifted to me. Every person on earth has been endowed with extraordinary and individual gifts, ideas, and aptitudes.

But this endowment comes with responsibility. If it's true that you are unique, then it's also true that there is no one else like you. That means you have something to give to everyone, something no one else can provide. You truly are the missing piece of the grand puzzle. No one else possesses edges like yours. I want to help you begin to see how your unique piece fits, because the more you understand, the closer you move to unlocking a life of alignment and fulfillment—a life where collaboration completes the picture.

From my Creator to my parents and teachers, as well as others who have influenced my life, I have received abilities, relationships, awarenesses, knowledge, and experiences that have become uniquely mine. You have a completely different collection. These make you as unique as your fingerprints and your DNA. Competition encourages us to hoard them, but you and I weren't created for competition. We were created for collaboration.

Awareness of my uniqueness changed the way I see the world. I began to look at everything around me and see the difference it made when I gave my unique ideas and abilities away. This unlocked a true vision of the emergent: the properties or behaviors arising from two or more things interacting with each other. I started to imagine what would happen when we combine two things, which is the very definition of creation.

As a teen, I saw the tractors and brush hogs sitting around the farm, my driver's license, and weed-ridden bank lots as resources. Combined, they gave birth to CGS—Chad's General Services (I didn't have quite the creativity around naming that I do today). Landscaping became my first official entrepreneurial effort.

Think about how the world would change if 8.2 billion people woke up every morning with a "give what you've been given" mindset? No longer do we worry about what we get, only about how we will add our unique piece to the puzzle.

This raises the questions: How much can I create by giving away what I've been given? What level of greatness could my ideas or abilities rise to if I were willing to put my piece into the world puzzle without focusing on the return? Or as Lee Brower, my friend who has touched the lives of many by giving what he has been given, poses it, "How much bigger would my world get if I became smaller in it?"

Moving Past Competition to Collaboration

As I said, the problem lies in the fact we have been rewired. Though the original manufacturer set us up for collaboration, people who thought they knew better rewired us for competition. But I would challenge you to see that competition is actually the obstacle. It's keeping you from reaching your highest potential.

If your only concern in school is competing with the other academic elites to become valedictorian, you might miss the opportunities giving brings. What if the person you collaborate with as their tutor has the Vision and Capabilities to start the next Google® or Amazon®? They simply need a math whiz to help them with the numbers.

In the workplace, "climb the ladder" and "corner office" have become common phrases. But ladders have only enough room for one person, and there are only so many corner offices. These mindsets create an atmosphere of competition. But what if the plan for exponential growth lies in the Collaboration Economy™, giving your best and combining your resources and assets with the people most would step on trying to get up the ladder first?

This is the Growth Formula: Growth equals Connections multiplied by Combinations ($G = C^2$). Everyone is connected to people, places, and things. Often these are combined accidentally to form collaborations. Imagine what happens when you begin to engineer them! Exponential entrepreneurs see every connection as an asset. Our intertwined lives are like the human body. When the parts of the human body stop collaborating and start competing, doctors diagnose us with an autoimmune disease or some other disorder. No one would call it natural. Yet, when we compete for grades, positions, jobs, status, wealth, or lands, the world applauds. Imagine the difference it would make in schools, organizations, workplaces, even countries, if we thought of every person or entity as a hand, a foot, an eye, or some vital organ, each supporting one another to the benefit of the entire body.

Think about it. The only competitions worth seeing feature winners who change from year to year. Most Americans love a good football or baseball game. Yet by the following season, the average person doesn't remember last year's stats. We love it when the most valuable players shake hands or hug after the game, because we know they understand the competition wasn't important. It was a game; they put their best on display, and everyone had a good time. The greatest athletes don't stay in the league because they win; they keep playing year after year because they love bringing their best to the field in collaboration with others who bring their best. In fact, when Tom Brady was asked by 60 Minutes how it felt to win all those rings, he said, "There's got to be more than this."[4] Interestingly enough, no team has won the Super Bowl® three years in a row. I believe the competition model leads to too many changes for long-term sustained success. Collaboration wins every time.

Exponential Entrepreneurs don't participate in competition that makes us hide our vision or hoard our assets because it isn't healthy or profitable. We can't put our best out there because we fear someone will steal it if they see it. Anything that hinders you from giving all you have without holding back is an obstacle to your growth and success.

Removing the Obstacle

When I was eight or nine, I felt like I'd been born in the wrong place. I love my family, and the lessons I learned on the farm are invaluable; however, I felt like I needed more stimulation. I thought my brain belonged somewhere like Manhattan.

But one day, a little light bulb went off. I realized that everything I saw was a simple math formula. Emergents were the result of combining two or more resources that already existed. If I could envision a new emergent, it would be the result of combining what already existed in a new way. That simplicity drove me to be quite curious. I began asking,

"Why does it work that way? How can I make this better?" I just had to figure out how to combine resources to create something new to answer my questions, and if the outcome was good, I made money.

All around, I see people who leak potential, but they can't collaborate with themselves. Too many people think their growth is restricted by their academic intelligence or effort. They've been told that everything good is outside of themselves, and they must go get it before they can provide any value to the world. They can't give because competition controls their resources and assets. I am here to share something you perhaps have never heard so clearly before: It doesn't start outside of you. You are the something special. It all starts with understanding your uniqueness and then applying it to what exists "out there." But you cannot do that if you continue to buy in to the competition mindset.

This idea of competition gets wired into us at a very young age. Our school system does the best it can, but grading on pure academics allows only a small percentage of children to excel. It bothers me how many children feel stupid because they don't fit the educational mold.

I encounter students who excel at math and science. Some don't share their knowledge because they fear what others will think, while others show off their brains, trying to intimidate colleagues. Both have been infected with the mindset of competition.

A teen who can't squeeze anything better than a C on a test sits in the same small group as those math and science students. She has powerful ideas that the science guru has been waiting to implement if she'd only share. But she keeps her visions to herself because competition for grades makes her feel less. The one who will be the town's most sought-after mechanic in ten years sits right next to the visionary. He knows he might not even graduate because of his scores, so he makes jokes and gets in trouble rather than contribute his technical skills to the group.

The teacher sees potential in all four. He knows greatness sits at those desks in front of him. He can feel it. But the competitive mindset, fear of what others think, and the lack of self-confidence instilled by competition lead to a mediocre project at the end of the week.

I was that student who underperformed. Much of the time, it was because I wasn't interested. I did the problem correctly once and didn't see the need to repeat the drill three more times. I didn't fit the mold of education; I saw life more from the light of "learn and apply to create."

Many kids are gifted in areas academia doesn't cover. They might not discover their assets until they get out into the real world, unless some adult helps them see that grades don't have currency. No one outside of an institution for higher learning will ever look past the fact you have a diploma. And while I don't want to give anyone an excuse to bring less than their best, we all know the person who graduated with straight Ds gets the same piece of paper as the valedictorian. So, why do we put this burden of competition on our children when we could be teaching them the beauty of collaboration?

But what if life is not a mold with limited space where everything that fills it looks the same? As I mentioned, I believe you are a distinct piece of a grander picture. And if life is nothing but a big old puzzle, and every person is a unique, integral piece, then when any single piece isn't in place, the picture isn't complete. That means there's no need for competition; there's a spot for everyone. You just have to figure out how you fit in, how to give what you have been given, and how to put your uniqueness in the place that causes the world to make a little more sense.

What if children were taught this puzzle piece concept at a young age? How would mindsets change if each person recognized their unique shape and place in the puzzle? Could the young man who excels at math collaborate with the young lady who has mastered English? What if we taught the musician to collaborate with the person who loves history, and the scientist to collaborate with the young person who repairs engines in his spare time? What could they teach each other? How much would they learn to respect others' skillsets? This kind of culture could obliterate the competition mindset. What might happen if we set an expectation that a successful collaboration means each person's grade will increase by 10 percent in the subject they struggle with? I believe the Code to Collaboration could add an entirely new and exciting level to the education system.

The Second Key

Stop and consider the times each day you feel jealous or doubt someone else's capabilities. Acknowledge the instances when you say, "I can do that better." Each of these moments reveals the places you feel obligated to compete.

We can't fix something until we see that it's broken, so the second key is recognizing the places where your brain automatically jumps into competition mode. After you identify that mindset, you can begin to shift it. How would an Exponential Entrepreneur look at the same situation?

When you feel jealous, tell yourself you should be grateful to know someone with great talents. When you feel better than someone else, look for what they excel in, the places you can learn from the person, or see if they are open to learn from you.

Every resource on the planet just waits for the vision that will allow it to connect and create something new and of value. An Exponential Entrepreneur strives to identify the unique Vision, Capabilities, and Reach that a person, place, or thing has to determine where it can be combined.

When you begin to look for ways to give what you've been given, you'll be amazed at the mindset shift it creates. Focusing on the unique parts of you and any business you have gives you a competitive advantage to see the world without conventional labels and identify the resources at your fingertips that will allow you to combine and create. Transforming your mind from go-getter to go-giver will be one of the most life-changing gifts you ever give yourself.

Part Two: Inspire

Chapter Three

Learning to Collaborate with Yourself

John Maxwell says, "You cannot lead others until you first lead yourself," and "You can lead yourself at your best only if you invest in yourself first."

Toddlers quickly move from collaboration to independence. As parents, we want them to learn to do things for themselves. It's crucial for their development. It's this quest for independence that leads to competition. If I see myself as an individual rather than a part of something greater, I feel a need to best everyone and everything.

When we tap into what Dan Sullivan calls our Unique Ability®, and begin to understand our VCR assets (Vision, Capabilities, and Reach), a concept defined by my good friend Dean Jackson, we become magnetic. You don't need to compete anymore because you understand no one can be a better you than you.

When we show up to give from the perspective of creating value for others, we don't need people to understand or label us according to convention. When we lead from the position of creating value, we share our ability to see a bigger future and a better path to get there.

Understanding My Unique Ability

Going through the process of uncovering my Unique Ability was quite impactful, and I can't say enough about the amazing experience I had working with Julia Waller to define my secret sauce in such a concise way.

Identifying and naming your Unique Ability is an important key to moving from competition to collaboration. Humanity tries to grade each person's performance. "On a scale of 1-10 . . .", "I'd give that a 95 out of a 100 . . ." But when we begin naming our Unique Ability, we suddenly see everyone as completely different. I can't compare myself to Julia. I don't have what Julia has. I can't compete with Julia; I can only combine with her. Embracing this means your influence increases, your income multiplies, and your impact rises to exponential levels.

But too many haven't taken the time to uncover their most valuable assets: their Vision, Capabilities, and Reach. They spend so much time becoming independent and competing to reach the top that they lose sight of what makes them unique. And because we're built for collaboration, trying to be independent brings additional inner turmoil because deep down we want to belong to something bigger.

That's why an essential key to collaboration is learning to collaborate with yourself. Collaborating with yourself is where it all begins. It's the place where you begin to embrace your uniqueness. I would encourage you to never stop exploring just how unique you are. It's the only way you can truly give what you have been given and get more than you ever imagined.

Your Constant Question™

From even before we're born until we reach about seven years old, theta waves program our subconscious. The voices you hear before you're born, the way your parents communicate, watching how people congregate, social interactions at the hardware store—we download each event into our subconscious. Every experience is pressed into our brains like a vinyl record, creating an operating system that shapes the way we function. Sometime between our seventh and eighth birthdays, we download it like a mixtape that drives our daily behavior. I call it a program our subconscious constantly runs.

Not only does this programming mold the way we act, but it also sets our constant question in our subconscious. Your constant question is at the foundation of how you uniquely combine. It's what will allow you to see the emergents that come most naturally to you.

Though I didn't recognize it until I became fully conscious of who I am and how I connect the dots, I now know my constant question stems from my curiosity. I always wanted to find out why and how; I knew things could continually be made better.

Interestingly enough, every person who had extremely similar experiences, including you and your siblings, will have a unique constant question molded by their formative years, as well as by how they perceive those events.

By the time you're eight, your constant question shapes every interaction. Adults often wonder why a young person stays quiet when they're introduced to a new environment, but what they're really doing is processing. Without realizing it, the child begins evaluating their surroundings according to that unique question. That's why when you and a friend go to the same movie, one can be moved to tears while the other finds it hilarious.

For some people, their life experiences have molded the application of their constant question in such a way that they live in competition mode. Their question sounds like this:

- "Why me?"

- "How much will this cost?"

- "Why do I always mess up?"

- "How can I protect what I have?"

If those sound like the thoughts that go through your mind when you enter a new situation, the first step in learning to collaborate with yourself will be reprogramming your constant question.

You might not even be aware you have this constant question. However, you probably notice that something holds you back. For some reason, you can't become a go-giver. You feel like you have to prove yourself. Life feels like a big chess game. You need strategy and timing. You always have to think three steps ahead of your opponent because failure is not an option.

But that kind of mindset will wear you out and rob you of the possibility of becoming everything you were created to be. The first step to unlocking the Code to Collaboration will be activating your Collaborative Intelligence™ by applying your constant question's power to leverage collaboration over competition.

Working with Julia Waller to uncover my Unique Ability helped me pinpoint my constant question. I highly recommend downloading Strategic Coach's *Beginners Guide to Unique Ability* to jumpstart your journey toward unlocking the Code to Collaboration. Better yet, if you're an entrepreneur seeking to grow, join Strategic Coach and let Julia help you as she assisted me.

When I saw my Unique Ability spelled out, curiosity invited me to find out where it came from and what the heck I would do with it.

It tracked me back to an awareness of the way I connected the dots when I was eight years old. Becoming conscious of my constant question morphed into understanding my Unique Value Contribution™ (UVC)—the practical application of the tens of thousands of different ways I answered my constant question. Every time you answer the question, every action you take, creates your unique way of doing things. The way you answer your constant question reveals your most authentic expression of value creation.

Dan Sullivan said when he began to consider his constant question, he could see the way it started to drive the trajectory of his life at age eleven. He can't help but wonder, "Just how far can I go?" Dean Jackson is one of the world's biggest simplifiers. His constant question is "So, what should we do now?" He takes that simple question, along with "Why should we do it?" Then, he simplifies.

Both of these titans have shown up in the world to give what they have been given, and they've impacted people all over the planet—many more than if they had lived with a competition mindset.

Even if your environment caused you to frame your question in a competitive tone, by activating your Collaborative Intelligence, your question can become what drives a go-giver.

Everyone I've talked to about this idea of a constant question has looked at it with speculation at first. However, when they took time to explore it, every person found the question that drove their actions.

I want to help you uncover your constant question. It's a program you've been running for a very long time, and some who uncover it even consider turning it into a product, service, or business. If you'd like to dive deeper into your constant question, check out the video on YouTube by scanning this QR Code.

Accessing Your Supercomputer

Shifting your mindset will allow you to collaborate with your intelligence. It will grant access to the subconscious so the conscious can work in tandem with it. Your subconscious is a supercomputer. It drives 95 percent of your behavior every day. But until you become aware of your constant question, you can't leverage the power of that supercomputer.

To give up the competition mindset, we have to develop an awareness that lets our conscious and subconscious collaborate. If we want to control the outside, we have to be in authentic connection to the inside.

Your first thoughts every morning can give you insight into your subconscious. If you wake up worrying about the day, making lists of everything you have to get done, or finding negativity before it occurs, you probably live in a competition mindset. Fortunately, our brains were made to be molded. With a bit of intentionality, you can shift those subconscious thoughts and create new habits that will give you a collaboration mindset.

I use my Daily GRACE™ model to set my brain on the right track. Throughout the day, these five practices keep me centered:

- **Gratitude:** Before I open my eyes, I start naming all the things I'm grateful for. This intentionality reprograms my subconscious so I can be in collaboration with it as it drives my conscious. Since we can only work with what we've been given, I need to know what I have to work with. This time of gratitude allows me to see those gifts more clearly. Until I started this practice, I couldn't be my best self.

- **Reflection:** I read and reflect several times throughout the day. My morning routine has about half an hour set aside to reflect on meaningful meditations, and in the evening, I dive into other books.

- **Awareness:** I spend the day being intentionally aware of what's going on around me, attempting to focus on being the observer. I try to pay attention to my internal reaction and how my past experiences shape it so I can understand my feelings before letting my reaction become a reality.

- **Create Value:** I am addicted to creating value for my family, myself, and others. When I see friction, my brain looks for solutions. We create value by simply giving what we've been given. I would go so far as to say being a go-giver and a value creator is what we were all sent here for. That's why creating value gives us great satisfaction.

- **Engagement:** I look for ways to engage with people or things throughout the day, so I can encourage others and create a grateful environment. Who am I going to give what I have been given today?

The Daily GRACE model allows you to unlock what you already possess internally. And the more you practice it, the more you begin to see what you have externally as well. Learning to put these practices in place can take time, but it will become the most valuable thing you do as you work toward unlocking The Code to Collaboration and start evolving into an Exponential Entrepreneur.

You Have a Vision

Today, someone sits in a cubicle at an office feeling like something is missing. Maybe it's you. Only the people in the next two cubicles know your name. You feel insignificant.

But you have an idea.

You might not realize it, but deep down, you're an entrepreneur.

Do you remember the definition of an entrepreneur? Someone who takes resources that perform at one level and moves them to a higher level.

When we encounter friction and find ways to alleviate it, we can track backward to understand the simple combination formula that results in the current reality. Then we can recombine what exists to produce a higher or better outcome. Even those who will never start their own company have the potential for an entrepreneurial moment, even an entrepreneurial life. Unfortunately, we let our competitive wiring get in the way of combining our VCR with someone else's.

Competitive wiring hoards imagination and abilities. It instills a fear of someone stealing our vision or abusing our abilities. It convinces us we need to protect our ideas and skills. After all, the competitive mindset assumes other people might not think our ideas or skills are as good as we believe they are.

Because society has wired us for competition, we forget we were built for collaboration. Competition mode adds stress to our lives because we remain vigilant, watching for ways to get ahead. We see enemies all around and spend a great deal of time frustrated because we have ideas and capabilities that don't go any further than our front door. We sense we were made for something bigger, but we can't seem to reach it.

For many years, I searched for ways to grow. I saw friction, and I found a way to resolve it. Usually, that meant I validated the size of the market and started a new company. I'm here to tell you that kind of thinking puts you in the slow lane of the interstate of entrepreneurial growth. After I finally realized that when I focus on what I already have and recognize each asset as something to give, a world of possibilities began to open.

Stop Deleting the Future You Want™

Sadly, many limit their awareness of these possibilities. Every person receives a massive number of inputs every day. Some estimate we process 2.2 million bits of information every second. Fortunately, our unconscious brains are great at deleting what we don't need. While our subconscious continues to process all that, it only passes to our conscious mind what we can handle—less than 200 bits per second. Just to put that in perspective, we process a minimum of 40 bits per second just to carry on a simple conversation.[5]

Remarkably, if a half-dozen people all take in the same 2.2 million bits of information, each one will process a different 200 bits. Only one second passes, yet the moment produces six perspectives based on the information the individual subconscious mind passes to the conscious mind. Imagine the possibilities over minutes and hours.

Living with a competition mindset stops us from keeping the right bits of information. We don't accept everything we've been given. Because we feel hesitant to share, we don't believe it's possible that so much could be given to us. We don't see the resources around us or in us. Ideas get stifled because we're on high alert, watching for what others are doing. We end up deleting the most productive inputs and miss the excitement of combining and the benefits of collaboration. I tell people all the time, "Stop Deleting the Future You Want."

Name Your Vision

One of my favorite things to do is help people retain the inputs that will allow them to collaborate. I want everyone to realize the uniqueness of their visions, strategies, processes, and offerings. If you feel limited by your academic achievements, I want you to know it's not your intelligence or your effort holding you back; it's the clarity of your vision and the quality of your collaborations.

The first step in recognizing your uniqueness is to name it. Naming your unique visions and processes not only allows you to stop deleting the future you want, but it also makes it easier and faster for other people to see value and feel safe with your idea.

When you name your uniqueness, it dispels confusion. When I can process something quickly, I can move forward. When I have to look for meaning, I process slowly. It holds me up, and I can't be as present as I'd like to be. Naming allows me to anchor meaning to the idea or object. By naming it, you make it easier for me to interact with you, and in some cases, to do business with you.

Think about it, the first assignment on Earth was naming. Genesis describes it. God told Adam to name all the animals. Immediately, the names removed confusion. Adam didn't have to describe the furry animal to get his point across. He could simply say, "I saw the cat."

After I considered all this, it became obvious to me that entrepreneurs could create huge value for themselves by naming everything that makes them and their business unique. In fact, I believe it's so important that I created a tool called Name the Baby™ to inspire you to do just that. It's a tool I give away at SEEDSPARK.com/tools.

Scan this code to access Name the Baby & other tools

But before you can name it, you have to recognize it. Exponential Entrepreneurs create value through vision, collaboration, and combination. And, they are not limited to their own Vision, Capabilities, and Reach. They open their minds to see everyone's VCR assets as something waiting to be combined to create. They understand that imagination is prime capital, no matter who has it.

Every person on the planet has a vision. And the way you do what you do to bring that vision to life is your secret sauce. Sadly, almost every entrepreneur I am introduced to is giving their secret sauce away for free. Their invoices look the same as those of someone across town or across the country. But they don't need to give it away for free. People are willing to buy from them because of the outcome they create, and they do that in their own special way. This unique way of bringing your vision to life needs a name.

I've discovered that when I name how I do what I do, it's easier to offer it to others. Believe it or not, a name also signals that your process is safe. Since prehistoric times, our internal systems have kept a constant vigil to keep us secure. I know it sounds small, but think about the brands you buy because you know their names. You don't wonder or speculate. The unknown forces us to spend time in every interaction to make certain we'll be safe. And after we confirm the transaction is safe, it's valuable. Naming matters.

Naming your secret sauce also empowers those you serve to become ambassadors for you. Without a name, your idea has no anchor. Your potential ambassadors can't communicate a series of bullet points. It's difficult to perceive value from a list of benefits. Naming possesses power. That's why it was the first human assignment in the Bible.

I name everything. When I work one-on-one with entrepreneurs from around the world, I call myself the Chief Collaboration Officer™, and I named my worldwide collaboration community The CoLAB by SEEDSPARK. The operating system all CoLAB Partners use to create unlimited value for others and themselves, we dubbed CoLAB OS™. Every collaboration tool I create, everything I have to give has a name.

This can be equally powerful for you. Names make it easier to collaborate with yourself. Once something is named, it can't be unseen, perhaps because names make your visions real. We generally only name living things or non-living things with great value. Now that you can see the pattern in what already exists, it's time to start leveraging it for yourself.

Collaborating with yourself gives you the ability to combine what you see with what you know to provide value for other people. Every time you combine, you create—for yourself and others. Only one person can do that the way you do: you. Collaborating with yourself gives you a wildly different outcome.

Identifying, knowing, and being yourself allows you to enter the world giving only what you've been given, while doing it in a collaborative way. You will be able to fulfill dreams you haven't even dreamt yet. Collaborating with yourself opens doors. You listen to learn and understand rather than listening to respond. You become confident in who you are and what you have to contribute. When you approach the world this way, you open up the subconscious and create an amazing impact.

The Second Key

We all believe every child has been made unique with special gifts. They are an expression of the divine here on earth, having a human experience. Why do we forget that when we get past eighteen?

Perhaps because we were never told we were each uniquely designed to create value in the world. You can only give what you've been given, but when you show up to give it—not hyper-focused on what you can take, but genuinely looking for a way to give back—the world is unlocked.

Believing this truth is the second key to the code.

So, what holds us back? Why can't we collaborate with ourselves? The competition mindset is your obstacle, and your constant question might be what's trapping you. But don't give up! I've met many people, and even some of the world's most successful entrepreneurs get stuck. You might need help getting out of the quicksand of competition and a negative constant question.

In the next chapter, I'm going to tell you more about my friend Dr. Stelios Nikolakakis. Though he needed some help defining his Unique Value Contribution when I met him, he has now fully embraced his Soul SIGHT^{IP}, which helps the highest performers on the planet get unstuck. With a little coaching and a proven framework, you can overcome the obstacles, learn to reframe your constant question, and see the ways you personally were uniquely designed to create value in the world. You can discover your own Unique Value Contribution.

You and your assets are valuable just as they are. You already have everything you need to create all you ever wanted. When you learn the art of collaborating with yourself and combining your numerous assets, you will unlock personal empowerment and achieve far beyond your dreams. When you start loving what you do, combining your Vision, Capabilities, and Reach, and collaborating with yourself and others, you will increase your Collaborative Intelligence. People might call you a go-getter, but that won't be true. You will begin turning your purpose into a platform. Exponential Entrepreneurs who reach those heights are truly go-givers.

Before you move forward, take a minute and pick out three memorable events from your life. You will immediately see each one involved in combining what you have with another person, place, or thing. If we allow ourselves, we begin to see all of life as a collaboration.

Chapter Four

You Already Have Everything You Need to Create More than You Will Ever Want

Magine walking along a beach and picking up every single thing you pass. You find beautiful shells, shark's teeth, sea glass, driftwood, crabs, and other delightful ocean gifts. But you'll also find trash left behind by others. Of all that you collect, how much will you keep in your bag, and what will you throw in the next garbage bin?

As we walk through life, collecting happens naturally. This morning, you woke and immediately began collecting. As I explored what drives some to excel more than others and how collecting influences it, I looked backward into all that has been and reviewed what exists now—where I am. Then, I looked at the additions and subtractions that filled in that period through relationships, awareness, knowledge, and experience that brought me here, and I started to see this formula. It is this simple pattern of collecting that separates us. Some do it naturally, others must do it more deliberately. Every day we're given, we collect beautiful things we should treasure. I created a process to help find the things we collect to take action on. I call it RAKE, because the items that provide unlimited opportunities to create can be broken down into four categories:

- Relationships

- Awareness

- Knowledge

- Experience

Sadly, we don't journey through life with the same anticipation as when we're near the ocean, and because we aren't attentive, we hold on to things we should throw in the garbage and delete the things that make us entrepreneurs and collaborators.

Your RAKE Gives You Unlimited Opportunities to Collect, Combine, and Create

Hopefully, by now, you believe that there is no one on Earth quite like you. I'm convinced you were given your uniqueness to create uncommon value. You see things other people don't see, and you look at things from an extraordinary perspective. When you learn to collaborate with yourself and understand your Unique Value Contribution, you begin to be more deliberate in your collecting and pay attention to the things around you that fit in your RAKE because you know they provide the key to The Creation Code^{TM}, or your IC3—your ability to Collect, Combine, and Create. This methodology has served as a catalyst to get more than one entrepreneur unstuck and creating.

Scan this code to access the IC3 tool

You can leverage your RAKE by simply looking back over your calendar. You'll find unlimited opportunities to create from what you Collect there. When we take everything we Collect in our RAKE every day and Combine it with who we know, what we know, and where we know, we can Create things never before imagined. But first, we have to learn to inventory our daily meetings with Relationships, Awareness, Knowledge, and Experience. Most days you'll get all four. The highest performing creators I know absorb these and do one thing differently than those who never reach their full potential, but I'll tell you more about that later. Most importantly, they become very intentional about shaping the way they perceive their inputs.

Collect

Every day, high performers look for the Relationships they form or build. When I looked backward, it became clear that Relationships played a huge part in the addition and subtraction that made up my present. Paying attention to the relationship created in your wake, combined with the IC3 Formula, unlocks everything of exponential value. Maybe you had a new waiter at your favorite restaurant or got an opportunity to talk one-on-one with someone on your team that you rarely get to meet with. No encounter goes unnoticed for someone collecting ways to create value for others. Later, we'll look at how recognizing the uniqueness of every individual empowers your ability to become a value creation factory.

The next thing you collect in your RAKE is Awareness. When you begin to leverage what's been given to you, you will notice a heightened sense of Awareness. You pay more attention to every detail. Taking a recount of your Awareness at the end of every day can help shape the way you combine things.

Knowledge is different than awareness. Looking backward, I could spot many times when I discovered the way to do something, how things originated, or why something was the catalyst for something bigger. Do you read or listen to podcasts every day? How do you take in new information? Every bit of data you come across has the potential to give you Knowledge. Believe it or not, I like to create short book reports for myself. Every time I read a book, I create a file on my computer with my greatest takeaways—the things that gave me more Knowledge. And I share those insights with many entrepreneurs around the world, because that's what it means to give what you have been given.

The final aspect of your RAKE is your Experience. Every moment offers unique experiences that shape your perspective and feed your creativity. Whether it was a meeting with someone new, visiting a place with new tech, a trip to a new city, or time spent with someone you care about, each moment offers experiences that shape your RAKE.

By using your RAKE daily, you'll find the resources you need to combine and create. I encourage you to take out your calendar and look back over the past week or month, or perhaps years, and make a list of your Relationships, Awarenesses, Knowledge, and Experiences. Then, update your RAKE daily so you don't forget anything. Some days, you'll fill in only one blank, and others, you'll fill in all four. But I guarantee the more you look for what you caught in your RAKE, the more often you'll find gold. Intentionality is key.

Did I mention I love to create tools? You can access one to help you as you use your RAKE by scanning the QR code to the right.

Combine

With all the inputs we receive every day, people around us could wake up in the same house, go to the same meetings, receive the same emails, eat the same lunch, and end up with stories that tell of wildly different experiences and outcomes. Think about the last movie you and your spouse or friend saw together. Though you spent ninety minutes enjoying the same experience, you each walked away with an enormously different perspective.

Combining the different perspectives gives you a more complete picture. The same thing happens when you combine the perspectives you find in your RAKE. Suddenly, the picture emerges in 4D.

This ability to combine distinguishes ultra-high performers from traditional performers and even high performers. There it is, the most powerful collaborative word: Combine. Fortunately, it's a skill everyone can develop. By now, you've begun to embrace your uniqueness, and you're starting to see how powerful your UVC makes you.

Create

Now it's time for magic to happen. Using your RAKE and The Creation Code can help you develop new and often exponential emergents. When this becomes your default programming, you will begin to see many ways to create unlimited value for others.

That's the secret to value creation: give it away. When you show up as a go-giver rather than a go-getter running from The Creation Code, the world opens up to you. Possibilities you can't imagine begin to surface in your life. This is when your path becomes non-linear—not because you put in more effort, but because you have begun to see and operate more naturally. When we create out of the unique way we were made, we reap the benefits of getting things done with less friction.

By applying the strength of collecting, combining, and creating, you will see new and unique value without limits. That's why collaboration gives us exponential power. When I combine the limitless value from everything I collect in my RAKE with the limitless value you've created with your RAKE, the prospective outcomes reach infinity and beyond.

Unpack It

My RAKE gives me the opportunity to Collect, Combine, and Create. For instance, I go to the gym every morning. I use the sauna, steam, and cold shower (ouch), and move forward in my day with my daily strategic assistant meeting. So, when I showed up one morning and experienced an out-of-order sign on the door of the sauna, my mind automatically began to Collect, Combine, and Create.

I'm aware that my gym has a tremendous app with texting capabilities, and that usually, the sauna has several people in it when I'm there, so it's well used. I've also connected with the wonderful maintenance crew. Within a few moments of collecting and combining all the details, I created a simple solution. When the maintenance department put the sign on the sauna door, they could or should also have had the power to send a message via the app to alert all the clients that the sauna was down. They already have all the components in place, and a great way to create value for their clients and avoid attrition would be to let them know when any piece of equipment isn't available. And the beauty of the plan is that they can do it by simply combining what already exists.

I constantly tell my daughters, "Complainers don't create, and creators don't complain." So, I took a moment and collaborated with my gym. I sent them a message with my value creation. I gave them the vision I'd been given. You might think I'm not getting any part of the outcome; however, the next time a piece of equipment I regularly use is unavailable, and I'm able to rearrange my schedule to be more efficient because they notify me, I'll receive my share. I can always use more time, and I am pretty sure many of you are the same.

Imagine how much loyalty your favorite business could build by creating a way to keep you updated on things that might disrupt your schedule. And if you have an idea to accomplish it, why not become their collaborator, share it, and split the outcome? While these kinds of C3s are the baby steps of collaboration, they illustrate how giving rather than hoarding our Vision, Capabilities, and Reach creates value that will inevitably benefit you. Imagine a world where everyone had this mindset!

I naturally see the emergent—the outcome from combining two or more people, places, or things. Nearly every day, I am introduced to something new. Immediately, I combine this new idea with something that exists. This method of combining allows me to create collaborations for entrepreneurs all over the world on a daily basis. The Creation Code is my way of helping others step into this realm I naturally live in. Your RAKE will help you discover that you already have all the components you need to make magic happen. Recognizing what's all around you—Collecting—and then putting those things together—Combining—will become a game-changer for you to create value for others. Because Collecting and Combining naturally births Creation.

Your RAKE Is Your Key

It's not often that entrepreneurs come to me feeling they have nothing; however, sometimes they'll have blinders on that only allow them to see the industry they are in. They put limits on what they can Collect, Combine, and Create. When they remove the blinders, they discover they've been deleting the most productive inputs. One of the keys to creating the future you want is to collect, combine, and then create something that helps others get the future they want. By embracing The

Creation Code, you will see that you have the ability to create unlimited value and become the guy or gal everyone loves.

Don't let another day go by before you start using your RAKE. Keep track of your Relationships, Awareness, pieces of Knowledge, and Experiences every day. Then look for ways to combine them.

Steve Jobs said, "Creativity is just connecting things. When you ask creative people how they did something, they feel a little guilty because they didn't really do it; they just saw something. It seemed obvious to them after a while. That's because they were able to connect experiences they've had and synthesize new things. And the reason they were able to do that was that they've had more experiences or they have thought more about their experiences than other people. Unfortunately, that's too rare a commodity. A lot of people in our industry haven't had very diverse experiences. So they don't have enough dots to connect, and they end up with very linear solutions without a broad perspective on the problem. The broader one's understanding of the human experience, the better design we will have."[6]

I don't think high performers need to have more experiences to be creative, but I would say they need to intentionally recognize not only their experiences but their entire RAKE. And more importantly, they look for ways to combine.

Every day, I tell someone that Vision is the catalyst. You are an Exponential Entrepreneur with ideas and imagination. Take that and combine it with who you know, what you know, and where you go, and your RAKE now has more dots to connect than you ever imagined. Today's the day to begin Collecting, so you can Combine and Create.

Chapter Five

Collaboration Currency

Before you can give, you have to know what's in your own wallet. And I am not talking about your Capital One® card. You have something way more valuable. Fortunately, we all have a currency that goes beyond dollars, euros, pesos, and yen. Every person on the planet has Collaboration Currency™. But too many people don't know what's in their account, and when you don't know your Collaboration Currency, you are earning the worst interest rate possible on your potential success! Someone who doesn't know what's in their bank account cannot be a generous benefactor.

Did I mention your parents were right when they said you were made unique? No one else has your childhood, your experiences, your family, your relationships, and your individual talent and ideas. Understanding that simple principle is vital to determining your Collaboration Currency. I spend a great deal of time every day talking to entrepreneurs. One calls himself a plumber. Another has the title "litigation attorney" on his business card.

Similarities don't create Collaboration Currency. Whether you have your own business, work for someone else, or are a student sitting in a classroom, the way you create value is completely different and unique from any other person on this planet. You have more value to contribute than you realize.

It's this value that gives you your true identity—not your job description, not even your name. And embracing your identity is the first step to becoming an Exponential Entrepreneur. I love helping people discover their unique Vision, Capability, and Reach. These are assets we all have, but first you have to learn to inventory those assets and see the assets of others as something to combine for the benefit of creating value. You've been told how special you are. Leveraging these assets is the unlock. This is your Collaborative Intelligence (CQ). You have this power inside just waiting to be unleashed.

Collaborative Intelligence will allow you to move beyond knowing you are special and unique, into using your extraordinary value to make this world a better place. Gaining CQ is the link that will take you to freedom of Vision. It will give you the ability to live, create, and build without constraint.

But first, you have to inventory your VCR assets so you can give them a name and find ways to combine and share with others, splitting the outcome. Inventorying your VCR assets fills your wallet with Collaboration Currency, and naming it gives it life. It tells the world you recognize your value, and neither you nor the world will ever be able to unsee it.

VCR Is Your Collaboration Currency

I know why you haven't acted on those Visions you've been receiving. Like most, you don't have the Capabilities. And even if you have some resources and enough cash to buy the rest, you don't have Reach. That's why the Code to Collaboration is your life's unlock. It's the secret to more exponential growth than you can imagine. I hope you are beginning to see that you and all the parts of you are the missing piece to someone else's puzzle, and the missing piece to your puzzle is found in collaboration. I know. It sounds too simple, but it really is! The reason you exist today in your current condition and location, doing what you do, is a simple math formula of items collaborating with one another. There's the power. To change anything about you, you simply change one or more of the elements that are currently collaborating in your life formula.

Dean Jackson, who is also my CoLAB Partner, developed the VCR Formula to help him understand how exponential outcomes keep happening. It's the key that creates the foundation of your Collaborative Intelligence. The book we worked on together, *The VCR Formula*™, explores it in depth, but the simple explanation is this:

Vision + Capability x Reach = Success

Perhaps you have a unique Capability. It might look like someone else's on the outside, but deep down, you know the way you do it is different than anyone else. When you add another person's unique Reach or Vision, you can create something bigger than you ever imagined.

Think about the last beautiful building you were in. That happened because someone had a vision and found a uniquely skilled architect and contractor. Without all the components, we would never have that tremendous structure.

However, the building sits empty until you multiply it by Reach. This is where amazing things happen.

Take Richard and Maurice McDonald, for example. These brothers had amazing Capabilities and Vision. They saw a way to bring quick meals to the average working person. Their Speedee Service System is the basis for every fast food restaurant you visit today. But without Ray Kroc extending their Reach through franchising, no one outside of Southern California would know about it today. For fifteen years, the brothers operated their single McDonald's® in San Bernardino. By the end of their fourth year of collaboration with Ray Kroc, there were 1,000 restaurants. Eighty years later, it's difficult to keep track of the number of McDonald's, because the franchise opens and closes hundreds of sites globally each year.[7]

Richard and Maurice's Vision and Capabilities made them a nice income. However, Ray Kroc's ability to duplicate their success and put Reach into play has multiplied their success many times over.

Every day, someone has Vision to add to someone else's Capability and multiply with another person's Reach. The possibilities are immeasurable. Better still, everyone has some portion of each in their own portfolio of VCR assets. And when you activate them by showing up to give and then split the outcome, the combination in your arsenal becomes your Collaboration Currency. No more investment, no more risk, no more effort, you simply show up with what you already have to give and combine it with someone else's VCR. Operating this way is not a 10x strategy; it's 100x and sometimes even 1000x. So where do we begin?

Vision

There is no shortage of ideas on the planet. This generation is quickly moving into what I call "The Collaboration Economy." Since the beginning of time, humanity has seen value in completed tasks. When the job is done, we write a check. Some will say, "Everything is in the execution." But I would argue, "What are you executing on?"

Vision is the catalyst. The person executing couldn't have done a thing without the Vision. It doesn't matter how grand the Capability or Reach is; without the Vision of how to combine what already exists, everything stalls. Consider the statue of David. Do you think Michelangelo saw the Vision of the statue, or did he simply knock off chunks of stone and voilá, David appeared? How about the Statue of Liberty? Did the French just throw metal together?

Every master craftsman leads with the awareness of how to combine what exists. The hammer, the nail, the wood, the saw, the chisel, the marble—everything needed to complete a beautiful, intricate design existed before the artists saw it. Vision brought them all together. Every innovation you see today is a result of using The Creation Code to collect things that already exist, combine them, and use Vision to create. Creating is all Vision, and it's all a collaboration. Even SpaceX and the other endeavors we see Elon Musk working on today are a result of collecting, combining, and creating from what already exists. Musk constantly expands his vision to push the world to new levels of The

Creation Code that have the potential to put humans on Mars and beyond.

Up until about third grade, we thrived in the Collaboration Economy. Our imaginations ran as free as our toy soldiers that charged up the hill and tasted as good as the imaginary tea we poured from our teapots. We had friends no one else could see, and ideas flowed from us without restriction. Then, sometime around eight years old, we moved from divergent thinking to convergent thinking. We fell into line and focused on tasks rather than the limitless vision of possibilities.

This means that when inventors introduced automations that took a great deal of the load off the workforce, humans started to worry about being replaced. Convergent thinking saw the machines as competition. In the last century, that fear has become even more prevalent. What will humans do when machines and artificial intelligence take over?

If we look back over history, from the beginning of time until today, we see the multitude of times someone has taken something that already exists to create more than existed before. That's what human beings do. We thrive and survive on combining and creating. We naturally don't fit into boxes. Conformity and "follow the leader" are learned behaviors. These mindsets train us to give up our curiosity. They are also mindsets that pay the leaders very well.

Through embracing the Code to Collaboration, you can return to your natural curious and creative state. You'll discover that AI is part of your RAKE. Artificial intelligence and machines become fuel for your engine that will power you to create the way only you can.

I have good news. You came factory-installed with everything you need to survive in an automated society. We just have to push past the shift that hindered our imagination and embrace divergent thinking again. Your vision and ideas have astronomical value. The trick is recognizing and combining them.

I explored my favorite tools for energizing Vision in my first two books. Curiosity drove my earliest ideas. I talk about the power of questions like "why," "how," and "what if" in *Just Add a Zero*. And as much as most people dislike it, friction is my second tool. Problems, grievances, and annoyances have been the source of some of humanity's most impressive inventions. Electric cars, underground tunnels, life on other planets; are you starting to see a pattern? Yes, you too can harness friction and collaboration to change the world. You can find more details about putting your frustration to work in *Friction Fuel*.

I bet curiosity and friction have triggered your imagination more than once. Unfortunately, most people dismiss their ideas because they lack a framework to activate them. They need the Code to Collaboration. Convinced no one will listen or that someone else is already working on it, they find all kinds of excuses to leave their Vision lying on the garage floor. And as you have likely seen, the idea moves on and becomes someone else's Vision to leverage collaboration. Do you remember seeing a commercial highlighting your idea?

I sense that I receive ideas from my imagination, which is directly connected to the field of possibilities. And after we receive these ideas, they seem to go through a process of gaining vision clarity. I define four levels of vision to empower global entrepreneurs, but they work for everyone. Clarity of Vision triggers action, and this vision analyzer helps me see which level my ideas are on and where I need a collaborator.

1. We start with **Fuzzy Vision.** Imagine an old black-and-white television with a rabbit-ear antenna. You can see your idea and begin to describe it, but it's just not clear.

2. After a time, you'll see it in **Color.** You can describe it now, but it doesn't have all the details.

3. But then, it moves to **HD.** Like a high-def movie, we can see shades, shapes, and shadows. You can smell it and feel it. It's not quite real yet, but the idea is beginning to come to life. And when it does:

4. It moves to **4D.** This is true visionary-level clarity. Not only do you see every detail of your vision, but you also see multiple paths to bring it to life. You can envision each person who will sit at the table when your idea becomes a reality, and everyone who will share in the outcome.

Everything we use daily started as an idea in someone's imagination as a result of curiosity driven by a friction. Everything. Take a moment and look around. Everything you see started in someone's imagination. Why not yours?

I recommend everyone has a vision partner. And when I say everyone, I mean that. Even I need a vision partner, someone who can walk with me through these stages and help bring clarity to the ways my visions can grow and create more value for my business or my life. SEEDSPARK and I serve as vision partners for some of the most successful entrepreneurs on the planet.

In my own experience, ideas automatically begin combining with internal and external inputs. Eventually, the idea becomes crystal clear. In fact, it has so much clarity around it, I tie an emotion to it. In that moment, the magic begins. Forward momentum increases because emotion lights the fire of ambition.

That's about the time my old pal friction shows up. This is where most visions die. Non-linear ideas and exponential outcomes attract a lot of friction, especially if you lack a network of relationships or don't understand the VCR Formula. Until you learn and activate the Code to Collaboration, the competitive growth methodologies you have been taught limit your ability to reach your true potential. Alternatively, knowing your VCR assets empowers you. Each friction becomes an open invitation for collaboration.

The problem starts because we're not taught collaboration. Understanding the VCR Formula allows you to see exactly how success happens. The person who made the chair that you sit in or the gadget that gives you comfort received a vision, but the vision doesn't become reality without collaboration. When we combine our visions with another person, place, or thing, we unlock magic. That's how we make things real and make them recur. We combine to cause an emergent.

I will let you in on a secret: one question you can ask to help move you forward is "Why not mine?" If everything starts this way and collaboration moves everything forward, why are my ideas not becoming something everyone already uses today? You guessed it. Collaboration.

People slept on the hard ground until someone recognized that straw or feathers stuffed inside a large sack would create a comfortable cushion.

Who was the first person to get tired of drinking clear water and decide to add leaves or beans? How long did civilization eat raw eggs before boredom asked "what if" and started cooking them? And what about the person who added meat, cheese, and vegetables to create scrumptious omelets? Every single advancement began as a vision in someone's mind. My question is, "Why not yours?"

The only difference between you and me is that you haven't taken action on your imagination. I tell people every day, "Capability and Reach are just waiting for your Vision to show up." If you don't believe me, do an internet search on any company name on the planet. They all have elaborate websites showcasing their Capabilities, and they desperately need your Vision to arrive.

When you begin to really see the power of The Creation Code in practice, you will start to see these businesses as ways you can be the Vision they are looking for. You have the ideas that will grow their businesses in ways they could have never dreamt of. The Creation Code empowers us to deliberately Collect, Combine, and Create for others, then step back and watch what happens to the go-givers.

I would argue that we receive Vision from the divine. Imagination is the gift of our Creator. When we get quiet and listen, ideas begin to flow through us. How many times have you needed to think, closed your eyes, and voilá, you could see exactly what you needed?

Oftentimes, when I'm in a group of entrepreneurs, I'll ask, "Can anyone create me a thought or an idea?" Humans don't have the capacity to make something out of nothing. We don't create ideas, we receive them. We have no choice but to take things that already exist and combine them. Our Vision is just one of the gifts that allow us to give back. The beauty in this is that since everything we need to implement our ideas already exists, everyone, including you, has the potential to be a creator.

It's time for humanity to embrace the unlimited ability we each have to bring our ideas and visions to life—to unlock our full potential with an easy-to-adopt mindset and a formula that harnesses everything you already have to create more than you ever want.™

Capability

We see Capabilities more easily than ideas. People with high-level skills spend a great deal of money showcasing their talent. Websites, sponsorships, and Facebook ads all highlight Capabilities.

However, Capability goes beyond skill. That's just the first type of Capability.

Every machine in your warehouse has one Capability individually and another Capability when combined with other machines. They might represent combined Capabilities not even close to what or how you currently use them. Your material inventory could be producing another Capability.

Imagine a farmer with a tractor that's only used during hay season. Another farmer down the road needs a tractor only during soybean season. The two could collaborate and split the outcome. Everyone wins.

I don't like to talk about people as commodities; however, every person in your office is a third type of Capability.

Suppose your business grows and you need to hire an extra person; however, you only have enough work to keep them busy thirty hours a week. Then you meet an entrepreneur with a tremendous Vision, but what they're missing is the funds to hire someone who can work two hours a day to get their Vision off the ground. Collaboration adds your assistant to their Vision and multiplies it by both of your Reach. All you have to do is decide how to split the outcome depending on the resources each of you contributes.

Today's convention trains us to sell our Capability to someone with Vision. The farmer could rent his tractor, and the entrepreneur could charge an hourly rate for his assistant. The marketing team will tell us they're selling to people who need their Capability.

A mindset that has activated its Collaborative Intelligence realizes the tractor is going to sit there whether the other farmer rents it or not, and you're going to pay your assistant's salary regardless of whether you choose to help the person with the Vision. It's not going to cost you a cent more to be a go giver.

On the other hand, a percentage of the outcome has the potential to be substantially more than the amount you can rent the tractor for or the assistant's hourly wage.

The fourth type of Capability should be more obvious, but few recognize it as such. Believe it or not, your cash flow is nothing more than Capability. It allows you to buy someone else's Vision, hire a consultant, or take someone's course or seminar. It also lets us chase others' capabilities, perhaps a marketing firm, manufacturer, or landscaper. And it lets us extend our Reach when we run ads on Facebook or sponsor a race team. I watch people with Vision set up crowdfunding every day. In a few years, they might be able to bring their idea to life. Alternatively, what would it look like if they collaborated with three or four entrepreneurs with the needed capabilities? They could start tomorrow and see their Vision realized within a few months rather than years. Would you happily split the outcome with other go-giver qualified entrepreneurs that you don't have to manage? We all look for talent with "batteries included" to reduce the amount of management and motivation needed. When you split the outcome, outcome and mindset manage behavior so you don't have to. It's just another benefit of thinking like an Exponential Entrepreneur and unlocking the Code to Collaboration.

Capability might be the most visible of the Collaboration Currency assets; however, increasing your Collaborative Intelligence will open your eyes to the value of the assets that surround you. Most entrepreneurs and people with a collaborative mindset discover they have a great deal of underutilized Capability. And when they activate that Capability in collaboration, every dollar the collaboration generates goes straight to the bottom line—more profit without the cost. The Code to Collaboration is the path to revenue before expenses.

When we start thinking about our Capabilities in the context of collaboration, we see visionaries who need what we have. They have a Vision to make the future better, and we can help them create something beautiful for the world.

Reach

Do you remember the VCR Formula? We add Vision and Capabilities, but Reach is the multiplier asset. You might think this is where you're most lacking, but whether you believe it or not, every person on the planet has Reach. Even someone on the corner in the hood has great Reach. Anyone with any kind of established trust relationships has Reach. These are the people who have confidence in you. You don't even have to say anything. If they see you like something, they'll consider it. And the more depth of Reach you have, the greater the impact of your Reach.

As a collaborative asset, we can leverage Reach to help someone else in their objectives to increase patronage and produce greater outcomes.

Maybe you're in college with an idea for a better sound barrier, or a stay-at-home mom with a new way to make babies comfortable, and you're thinking, "Who do I reach?" Your age and status don't matter; you have Reach, and now it's time to take inventory.

There are four types of Reach. Some have one; others have all four. We all have some:

- Eyeballs

- Minds

- Hearts

- DNA

The first layers of eyeball, mind, and heart Reach are easy to inventory. For instance, if your company sends out three hundred invoices each month, that's a small part of your eyeball Reach. Books, newsletters, and social posts allow you to influence the minds of your readers. The bang of eyeball and mind Reach has multiplied with the rise of social media. Every comment and thumbs-up allows you to track your impact. Even heart Reach can be counted by adding together the number of family, friends, and others who listen to you because you've touched their lives in a special way. Don't be afraid to think locally when you're taking inventory of Reach. You don't have to have the Reach of a Kardashian to take advantage of being the multiplier for someone else's Vision.

However, your Reach in each area is probably much greater.

If you have thirty service trucks traveling around the city, they log countless miles and sit in at least two neighborhoods every day. Those are really moving billboards with unlimited Reach. What if you gave some space on the side of your trucks to the pest control guy and split the outcome?

There's a barn in Belmont County, Ohio, that sits right along I-70. Every few years, the owner has a professional barn painter come in and create a lovely new scene on the long side. On the section that faces oncoming traffic, you'll see advertising for a motel or restaurant off the next exit. The entire end of the barn gets the eyeballs of 20,000 to 30,000 cars every day. Many farmers wouldn't see that as Reach, but at least one has found some Collaboration Currency and activated it.

One of my primary types of Reach is mind Reach. I have a team that takes my methodologies and puts them on LinkedIn every day. My ideas have the potential to cause an action in the minds and behaviors of my audience. A couple of hundred people comment. Heart Reach can spread to social media as well. If you've touched someone through thought-provoking posts, you have their ear.

Finally, there's DNA Reach. Finding this can take time, even for top-level entrepreneurs, but leveraging the Code to Collaboration can help you expand it. To find your DNA Reach, look for ways to serve your client's client. For instance, before Harvey Firestone and Henry Ford became good friends, they were collaborators. Firestone realized Ford's clients needed their product. So, he began giving what he'd been given and splitting the outcome. Ford's customers received the benefit of the very first pneumatic tires, and Firestone quickly became a major industry player.

What if you had a product or service that served those who drove Ford trucks? You could, of course, go and try to deal directly with Ford, or you could develop a relationship with someone who already delivers Ford products. Using this DNA Reach would collapse your time on the road to success.

What types of services do you offer that will improve the performance of someone who already has DNA-level Reach to people who need your product or service? Do you see how easy it is to create non-linear growth by leveraging the VCR Formula and the Code to Collaboration?

The key to Reach is making it easy for people to do business with you at scale. Sure, you can invest the time and money it takes to get your ideal client to know you, but wow, is that expensive. Then a little more time and money for them to figure out if they like you, and then some more time until they begin to trust you. And, if you hang in there long enough and have enough luck on your side, they might do business with you.

That's the conventional way. And you'll find countless playbooks on how to make it work. But I'm guessing you picked up this book because you are tired of slow growth, or you feel overwhelmed with the idea of starting your own business. I am hopeful you are beginning to understand just how capable you are of greatness, and that you're even more ready to start to leveraging the Code to Collaboration to create the future you have been destined for.

Calculating Your Collaboration Currency

The value of your VCR is limitless because the combinations are begging for the Vision to be seen. When we begin breaking down resources, it's vital to inventory every asset. Coaching might help people who need to grow their Collaborative Intelligence. For instance, if you've never considered cash as a type of capability or your entire contact list as Reach, someone with CQ can help you with your inventory.

But even with coaching, many have a difficult time with the Vision component.

Too many folks have spent their lives identified entirely by their job description, company, or industry. This means they miss the authentic expression of their assets and the value they can create by combining with others.

A landscaper sees himself as a guy who provides a service. But the landscapers I know can walk across the dirt and see the driveway, the trees, the pavers, and the monkey grass. To them, the land is a blank canvas where their imagination runs wild. Sadly, they only sell materials and labor because they haven't named their Vision and offered it as something people can buy.

What we learn here is that Vision is your most vital asset, and because your Vision's cost of goods has already been paid, when you activate it, it tends to be the area with the most margin. Naming it allows people to see it. Until then, it's invisible.

After building fifty-plus businesses and forming more than 1000 collaborations, I have never had anyone try to pay me for something that I hadn't named and priced.

More mature entrepreneurs recognize that their Vision allows them to keep contributing value much longer than they can do projects. Plus, the margins are 200 to 300 percent better. Are we in business to create exponential value or to follow the leader of best practices performance? I learned long ago best practices are still average, and I don't like average returns.

Remember, Vision is the catalyst. This is the gift I want everyone to open. Freedom of Vision removes limitations. Ceilings, industry norms, and conventional expectations become irrelevant. It's a gift you already hold in your hands; however, few ever unwrap it.

At some point, the landscaper will decide to retire and sell his operation. He can put a price on his equipment inventory, his cash flow, and his client list. But what made his company most valuable was his Vision. His clients appreciated the art he conceived, and this Vision is the reason they bragged him up to their friends.

The way you do what you do is the secret sauce, but so few sell it. As a rule, most of the population tries to grow through the conventions of their industry. They try to grow through more employees, offices, trucks, and square feet. They miss the value that their authentic expression and ever-expanding VCR assets actually create as exponential opportunities.

I want to empower the landscaper to name his Vision. If he does, he can continue to do the part he loves most—the thing he's been giving away for twenty-five years: his ability to see the final creation before work begins. Better yet, he can monetize it. He can collaborate with those who have the Capability, even the guy who buys his company. And because he has no cost of goods, the returns are wild.

Your Superpower

Another overlooked part of Collaboration Currency is the anomalous way you do what you do. If I looked at your home or your offices, your email signature, or your business card, they would all look very similar to those of others in your competition circle. Most invoices, names of services, and pricing stay the same across each industry.

However, the way you create value does not. You have patterns, habits, systems, and processes unlike anyone else. Those things you do that surprise people might be your most valuable asset. This is what I referred to when I told you about Dr. Nikolakakis finding his Unique Value Contribution. The spot where your VCR and Unique Value Contribution intersect is your Superpower.

I would like to share a little about a very successful entrepreneur who trusted my methods of non-linear growth for his outcomes. Robert A. Miller of RAM Pavement (RAMPavement.com) finds ways to collaborate every day, but people love to work with him because he does things differently. His P3 Program—Proactive Preservation of your Pavement Assets®—is just one asset that sets him apart. He collaborates with churches, shopping centers, offices, and anyone with a parking lot to proactively take care of their property. Convention in his industry repaves and repairs, but that's the most expensive approach to paving. His P3 Program lets these lot owners avoid huge repair bills in the future.

Another innovative practice that makes him an anomaly in his business is his Last Five Percent initiative. Talk about embracing the friction as a competitive advantage. Every truck in his fleet says "Last 5%" on it. In his industry, even the greatest companies leave behind the cones. Not only are the cones expensive to replace, but they are also an annoyance to the client who has to drive around them or move them before they can park. His Collaboration Currency includes his Superpower—making sure every job is 100 percent complete before his crews leave the sites, including collecting every traffic cone. His Collaborative Intelligence empowered him to recognize his Superpowers and name them. Everyone wins. Rob's clients have the best data and insights applied to managing their paved assets from two generations of wisdom. He wins because he builds deep, long-standing, trusted relationships, and he has a recurring revenue business model in a project-based business. Talk about building enterprise value in a non-linear way. Bravo!

On the day I turned around and introduced myself to Dr. Stelios Nikolakakis, I asked him about his occupation. He told me he was an optometrist, but then he began to tell me what he did. He showed me two pictures of a gentleman's eyes, the before and after. The photos contained only eyeballs, nothing else. However, except for the color, you would never have believed the eyes in the two photos belonged to the same person.

In the first photo, I felt like I could see through the man into nothingness. In the second, those same eyes were full of life and joy. "All this happened in just one session," Stel told me.

Now I was intrigued. I knew this optometrist had some serious Collaboration Currency that needed to be identified.

But Stel couldn't define what he did. Despite all his training and phenomenal results, he couldn't explain his process. He was a great deal more than an optometrist, but he hadn't yet started collaborating with himself to package his process and turn his purpose into a platform.

Stel had so much inside of him, but he had no idea how to package it, position it, message it, and offer it. He was definitely a go-giver, but he was giving everything away for free. When we unpacked his VCR and talked about his Unique Ability, he was able to define his processes and name them. He also identified a wealth of other professionals with their own unique VCR assets, and he simply started combining and creating. Today, a complete team of the best in their field collaborates. Dr. Nik and their collaboration, InVision, transform lives with their Superpower, a process he calls Soul SIGHT. I would encourage any entrepreneur who feels held back from their full potential to reach out to Dr. Nik (DrNik.ca). I have witnessed lives changing and dreams being exceeded. Bravo Dr Nik!

Without a clear definition of your secret sauce—your Superpower—you can't fully evaluate your Collaboration Currency. But even if you haven't named them yet, as you complete your VCR inventory, be sure to list those things that set you apart. Things like paying attention to details others overlook give you an advantage and make you more attractive to those looking for a collaborator. But don't forget the importance of naming. We want to make it easy for people to collaborate or do business with us. This seems to be the first rule of business that everyone forgets.

The VCR Key

Your next key to the code is developing an awareness that everything that exists on the planet is a resource waiting to be combined to create. We have to remove the labels and look deeper at everything around us. Nothing belonged to me originally; every resource I have was gifted to me—every Vision or idea, Capability, and person I know. And each time we combine resources, we create something better. Back when I was eight, I started to see horses, my ability to ride them, and my dad's dozen trips a month to horse auctions as resources. Combined, these three assets created an opportunity for an eight-year-old horseman's son to make a ton of money.

Leveraging Vision, Capability, and Reach assets through collaboration is what gives Exponential Entrepreneurs their unparalleled and non-linear growth. When you activate Collaborative Intelligence that recognizes and combines VCR, the results are greater than one person alone can imagine.

Scan to get your free chapter

If you would like to take a deeper dive into The VCR Formula, I invite you to check out a chapter of the book by scanning the QR code on the right. When you increase your Collaborative Intelligence, become aware of your Collaboration Currency, and show up to give it to others with Vision, Capability, or Reach, you will be able to not only split the outcome but also ignite the world.

Part Three: Ignite

Chapter Six

Don't Let Your Collaboration Get Lost in the Weeds

Many people I talk to about collaborating get hung up on things like risk and liability. They let questions spurred by fear and competition hold them back. But those are things you worry about in a partnership. Collaboration is different. In a collaboration, there's no risk because you aren't doing anything you haven't been doing all along. There's no competition because you're splitting the outcome—everyone wins.

The Difference Between Partnership and Collaboration

Many people use the terms 'partnership' and 'collaboration' interchangeably. They think collaboration is as simple as two people working together, but partnership and collaboration are wildly different. Some liken it to the difference between dating and marriage.

A partnership is like being engaged. It involves a mutual agreement between two parties—a buy-sell contract between go-getters. You can sue me, and I can sue you. When two companies partner, if one decides the partnership isn't working, like in dating, one can walk away, and both entities remain the same. In a partnership, we *do* something together.

In a collaboration, we *become* something together. Two or more go-givers combine their unique VCR assets to create something new, a creation that's never been done before. Something even more unique is birthed. Then they name it, package it, and promote it. One person has a Vision, and a second has the Capabilities needed to carry it out. When we add a third person's Reach, we have an amazing collaboration with more impact than any one of those three ever imagined. You don't have to worry about another person dropping the ball because their part of the investment is to continue doing what they've always done. Like in a marriage, the collaboration ceases to exist if one person doesn't show up, and neither party could have created the outcome without the other.

However, the best kind of collaboration goes beyond traditional thinking.

The most authentic expression of collaboration occurs when you take your Superpower and combine it with someone else's Superpower. When the two become intertwined, you have something new and wonderful that no one else, other than you and your collaborator, could have created.

Only the weaving of the musical virtuoso Richard Rodgers with the lyrical genius Oscar Hammerstein could have given birth to eleven award-winning productions, including their most beloved, *The Sound of Music*. Rodgers and Hammerstein brought the pinnacle of collaboration to the world.

Collaboration Lets You Break Up with Convention

We could continue to do things the conventional way—growth through more effort, more risk, more units for a similar return. We can even spend money on marketing or hire more salespeople. I think it's safe to say we all know how that timeline goes—you decide to expand, draft a job description, hire a recruiter, develop a compensation plan, field resumes…. Wait, we haven't even opened for business yet. First, we'll have to do training and ordering, and when we finally get started, we'll find all the places we missed the mark, start over, and burden our team, or we could try the non-linear, leveraged route.

How do things turn around when we start to focus on our Vision and impact? What have you been doing that you can do so much better? Fill in that blank with the name of the best entrepreneurs with that Capability. Next, figure out how much you need to keep from every dollar of that project to be satisfied, and split the rest among the names you wrote down. Now, share your Vision and participate in the outcome.

Did you notice how many steps you get to skip in the non-linear route? You are discovering the fast pass to the growth ride at EntrepreneurialLand.

The Code to Collaboration challenges us to break up with convention and find another unique person who serves our hero target.

A return to divergent thinking frees that mom with a Vision who creates a product to make her baby more comfortable. Then she combines with an online children's store where she and her hero target shops. This store has thousands of credit cards already on file. They've made it easy for people to do business with them. They don't buy her idea; instead, they collaborate to become the exclusive sellers. The mom continues to make her product, and the shop continues to sell products. But now the store has a new line, and if anyone engages, they split the outcome.

Famous world-class jewelers Tiffany and Co.® broke up with convention long ago. But to find their best collaborators, they have to invite people who share their hero target. This means looking for companies that serve clients who appreciate style and originality and also have deep pockets. In 2023, Nike®, and specifically their best-selling Air Force 1 shoe, fit the bill. Tiffany's AF1 '1837' features Nike's famous swoosh in the jeweler's signature Tiffany Blue®. Even the shoe box highlights the collaboration. With only 1,837 pairs made, they're priced between $400 and $6,000.[8]

Traditionally, the person with an idea finds someone with capabilities to bring their idea to life. The person with capabilities draws up a proposal. Conventional thinking completes the project and sends an invoice. Before the ink dries, interest rates go up and back down, a key person leaves, and everything changes. But this thinking aligns with competition instead of creating value. A simple modification in our thinking changes the game.

Collaborative thinking uncovers a way to modify how we engage with others.

From Competitor to Collaborator

Exploded View

Most business leaders have a definition of their industry. You hear the list at every networking event: I run a landscaping business. I built a restaurant. I own a marketing company. But with a highly developed CQ, you see things differently.

Most people see their business as a single entity. These leaders say, "I don't have anything to collaborate with." I challenge people from that group to reimagine their business like a diagram from IKEA®.

We've all seen those exploded views of furniture and engines. Each piece of furniture has hundreds of pieces, each with a unique purpose. Together, they make a bed, but until you fasten them permanently, the individual pieces have a life of their own. Your business works the same way.

That person who said they own a marketing company might have three photographers on staff, but they're only working in their Unique Value Contribution 25 percent of the time. When the marketing owner moves from convergent to divergent thinking, she picks up the phone and calls her competition. "Hey, turns out I have a photography company, and I'd love to collaborate with you."

Most business owners have never considered all the resources in their business that lie dormant. Like the extra screws that come with the IKEA furniture, they put their assets in a drawer because they don't fit the definition of your industry.

You have everything you need to create collaborations that surpass anything someone in your industry has ever put into action before. By giving your RAKE a broader sweep and recognizing your potential assets, you can offer even more value to others—and maybe even turn competitors into collaborators.

From Consumer to Collaborator

Most businesses also look at consumers as clients and customers, but what if we started to see them as pieces of the IKEA bed as well?

Meet Sam, a guy with great skills and capabilities, and Joan, a consumer who has an idea for something that will make her life easier. When Joan presents her needs to Sam, he sees something bigger than creating a new product for Joan.

"Miss Joan, I love your idea. I could create a proposal, and when we're done doing our best, you could write me a check. Or we could do something a little different," says Sam.

"What did you have in mind?"

"Well," Sam continues, "I think your vision is only going to get better over time, and I'm committed to making my capabilities better every day, too. I believe in learning as much as I can. I think we can make something better together. I've looked at my past work, and I have a little margin. Would you be willing to collaborate with me for 7 percent of the revenue? I will be responsible to own this portion of the overall growth. It's my sweet spot. I love your vision, and I would like to see us grow together and align for something bigger than a transactional project."

Joan, who originally just imagined getting her own project done, thinks this sounds amazing. "When do we start?"

"Today!"

Sam and Joan work out the details, they name it, decide how they will split the outcome, and agree to journey together using Joan's idea and Sam's abilities for as long as it works.

Conventional thinking would have given Sam one client for one day and would have allowed Joan to use her idea one time. Collaborative thinking allows Sam to offer his clients a great new product, and lets Joan make her idea available to her community. Their collaboration creates value, not only for Sam and Joan but also for the many who will benefit from their new creation.

I spent many years in a conventional, vertical-growth mindset. I got pretty good at making businesses bigger and extending my Reach. But then, I started to imagine how much faster I could grow if I looked left and right instead of within. The thought sparked Collaborative Intelligence. What would happen if I grew my business by helping the entrepreneur down the street grow hers? This collaborative mindset has exploded my outcome and increased my Collaboration Currency. Every time I enter into a new collaboration, I expand my Reach, increase the Capabilities available to me, and engage more people with unrivaled Capabilities.

Like a High-Performance Ferrari

Formula 1 racer Sir Lewis Hamilton understands using unconventional thinking to bring out the potential within. Nearly twenty years ago, he took the racing scene by storm with "one of the greatest rookie performances in F1 history." Since then, he has continued to win races and break records. But he does it by refusing to adhere to industry norms. Instead, he looks within, tapping into the best of what he's been given.[9] In fact, when someone asked about how he improved his Ferrari's performance, he had a surprising answer. "We've not moved the car forward in terms of performance, but there is more performance in the car that, if we execute a little bit better, I think we can extract more, so that's the goal."[10]

Like Hamilton's Ferrari, we all have more performance within. Whether you're an unknown living on a farm in South Carolina or you're an entrepreneur with ten or fifteen businesses, if we combine better, we can extract more. But you have to choose how you're going to execute.

Will you continue to perform at your current level, working hard alone to make a little profit, seeing small growth spurts through more effort, risk, hires, leases, and ads? That's the way it's always been done, right? Think about all those times your mom asked, "If all your friends jumped off a bridge, would you jump too?" You can stay on the same old treadmill of best practices, or you can embrace collaboration to hop on the autobahn of entrepreneurial growth. Let me tell you—growth on this side is much more fun and rewarding.

The Collaboration Flywheel

When I compare collaborative thinking to conventional thinking, one thing stands out—you don't have to work as hard to surpass your goals through collaboration. I see the constant striving in conventional thinking, and I'd estimate it requires about 80 percent more effort to reach the same outcome. That's why we call the ability to see your Collaboration Currency—and use it without limits—the Freedom of Vision. Now imagine accomplishing everything you're doing today using just 20 percent of the energy. What would that free you to do? What would it allow you to finally pursue?

I've known for years that I am not made for conventional retirement. I probably won't retire. I am addicted to value creation, and I absolutely love showing you and others how to do it and split the outcome. But knowing that about myself made me ask, "What am I going to do when I have the ability to do whatever I want?" I realized I would do whatever I desired. I wouldn't stop, but I wouldn't do things I didn't enjoy. What if instead of Retirement, your goal became Desirement^{TM}?

Desirement is where exponential alignment begins. It's living a life that aligns your desire, purpose, and collaboration to create the life you would choose again.

Sadly, most entrepreneurs live in obligation, as slaves to commitment, expectations, and identities they never consciously chose. Desirement is the process of returning to what you truly want and aligning your life, work, collaborations, and future around that deeper truth. In CoLAB, we strive toward Desirement by reconnecting entrepreneurs with their truest desires, authentic identity, unique design, purpose, calling, and future vision.

Below, you'll see the Internal Flywheel for CoLAB Partners. I call it a flywheel because when every part becomes activated, it creates unimaginable momentum. Developing Collaborative Intelligence is the first arm on the flywheel, and the first step toward giving yourself the gift of a Desirement Lifestyle™. CoLAB specializes in activating the entrepreneur's CQ. It's vital to grasp that message: You were born with CQ. It's in the building blocks of your DNA. Sometime about third grade, people stuck you in a competition lifestyle program and muted your CQ. It's been lying there dormant ever since.

But when you activate your Collaborative Intelligence, you develop the ability to see the connection between people, places, and things. The natural curiosity you had when you were five rekindles your Freedom of Vision. Suddenly, everything you see becomes something to be combined, and every combination brings an emergence.

Embarking on this journey to unlocking your Freedom of Vision means you are returning to your default wiring and programming. You begin to see the connections as natural parts of the equation. If you want to see a different outcome, you simply adjust the variables.

Freedom of Vision lets us run the scenarios and ignite our imagination. Ideas that were muted by the competition mindset of the world are unleashed. People start to look at us funny because we turn to non-linear thinking. They don't understand what we're talking about until after it happens, and then they wonder how we saw it ahead of time. You'll hear things like, "I would never have put those two things together." It's as if we found the umbilical cord that connects us to the divine.

You might remember that I told you our brains are great at deleting information that we don't need. Sadly, without Freedom of Vision, our brains also delete things we should keep. When you become fully aware of the power of collaboration, you begin to see that you are here to combine—that everything you need already exists. Embracing that knowledge allows you to revive the ideas you haven't implemented yet. You move from a "how am I going to make this real" mindset to a "this is going to be an amazing collaboration" mindset. Collaboration awareness encourages you to gain clarity. "How will my idea create real value, and who do I need to combine with?" Freedom of Vision connects us to all the possibilities the divine is trying to show us. When fully activated, it keeps us from deleting the future we want.

This Freedom of Vision allows us to evolve into a true Exponential Entrepreneur who sees all the existing connections as a means to move forward and live the Desirement Lifestyle.

The Desirement Lifestyle lies at the heart of the Internal Flywheel for CoLAB Partners. Activating your Collaborative Intelligence unlocks your Freedom of Vision, allowing you to see exactly how to move into action as an Exponential Entrepreneur with the ideas that have spawned in your imagination. This, in turn, drives further CQ growth, increasing your Freedom of Vision, spinning your flywheel faster and faster to create a world of limitless value creation by doing the one thing you never run out of energy for: your desires.

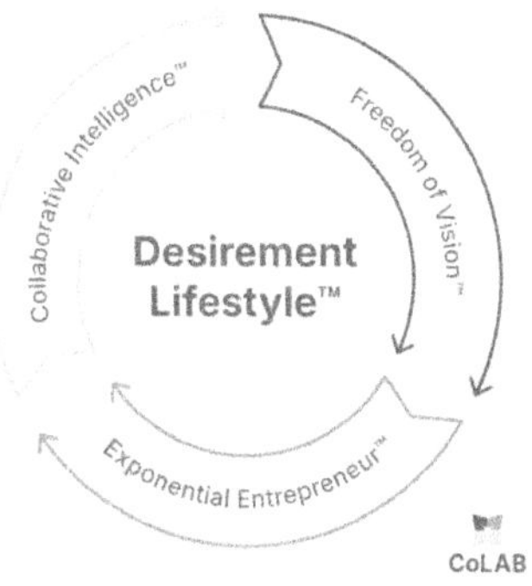

When we stop doing things outside our Superpower and focus on our secret sauce, Desirement begins immediately. Retirement has an age or tenure requirement. Desirement does not.

It's important to remember that living the Desirement Lifestyle is not indulgence. Desire gives you guidance; it's your future self sending you messages. When you listen to that inner voice, you'll find clarity in every dimension of your life: work, family, spiritual identity, creation, finances, and collaboration. Learning to live the Desirement Lifestyle allows you to move from what society taught you to want to what your original design tells you. It helps you understand the difference between desire and duty.

We don't have to wait until we hit that magic age or reach the perfect number in our investment accounts. We can create a schedule that reflects Desirement. Why not start today?

Empowering a Full Team of Entrepreneurs

But what would happen if you took collaboration even further and made it part of the fabric of your organization? People who've done it have seen monumental results.

The business owner who empowers his employees with the ability to collaborate begins to see the VCR Formula appear everywhere. When we treat employees as co-creators and team members, walls break down between departments, and job titles don't matter. When a company embraces the fact they are more than the sum of its parts, the opportunities to create value together multiply exponentially. It doesn't take long for Joey in the warehouse to engage with Jeff in engineering and Shirley in finance to create something that generates $1 million in new business the following year. How much smarter will all three work when they get to participate in the outcome?

Current business structures have layers of management designed strictly to oversee employee behavior. However, when you include those with the capabilities in your collaboration and develop a clear company-wide understanding of how each team member's uniqueness contributes to the overall outcome, you no longer have to manage your staff; the outcome manages behavior. Collaboration has the potential to attack the endless number of meetings—some of which are just to discuss having another meeting. There's a better way to do things. People endowed with an entrepreneurial mindset will voluntarily come in on a Saturday morning to meet a deadline and set aside time to increase the effectiveness of their unique value.

Today, SEEDSPARK approaches every project with the VCR method. We call it the CoLAB Operating System. We identify the Vision, Capabilities, and Reach components needed, and then the team selects the appropriate people to work on the project based on their awareness of who possesses the asset best suited for the outcome. This engineered collaboration produces phenomenal results with a fraction of overhead management.

Conventional thinking, labels, and titles trap employees in boxes. They become unable or afraid to share their ideas or unique capabilities because it doesn't line up with their title or position. Worse still, there's no incentive. The best of your team will end up leaving to start their own business. Even go-givers deserve recognition and compensation. They will only stick around and watch someone else take credit for and profit from their Vision for so long.

When the CoLAB-OS becomes your business model, it ignites innovation and value creation. You quickly see the difference between collaboration-based efforts and the traditional speed-to-market and retention concerns of commodity-based efforts. I've never met an entrepreneur who didn't want to have a self-managing and self-multiplying company, and CoLAB-OS is the how.

Determining the Outcome

As I mentioned, people get hung up on risk, liability, and other aspects that fall within the parameters of competition. One of the things go-getters worry about is splitting the outcome. But for a go-giver, the CoLAB Operating System is a simple concept to implement with just a little practice and support.

To get your head around it, think about your last profit-and-loss statement. If you mapped each logical line item to what you've learned about Vision, Capabilities, and Reach, you would see the range of how your VCR already shows up in your profit and loss categories.

Begin with Vision. It's easy to map to your net, or your bottom line, what's left after everyone and everything else splits the outcome. Then map the balance of your Capabilities—cost of goods and overhead—and Reach—commissions, bonuses, marketing, and sponsorships. While it varies by business, in the hundreds of collaborations and business models I've noticed a striking consistency in how every collaboration breaks down through the VCR formula:

Vision = 10-20 percent of the gross
Capabilities = 60-80 percent
Reach = 10-20 percent

This basic information empowers you to easily see how your business collaborates with your VCR. It also gives you what you need to leverage your contributions as well as the contributions of others, so you can begin to engineer your non-linear growth strategy and create exponential outcomes.

Imagine that someone with great marketing ability in the arts might meet an up-and-coming artist. The marketer can see the potential for income in the artist's designs, but because the artist is just starting out, he doesn't have funds to pay for the marketer's service on top of the advertising.

"I love your art!" The marketer tells the artist, "What do you think about a little collaboration? My fee usually ends up being five percent of an artist's revenue. How would you feel about paying the advertising bill every month, and then giving us five percent of your sales revenue? If it doesn't work out, you won't owe us anything more than the cost of the ads, but I think our audience will love your work. I actually think your work will go over so well, we'll make more over the long run than I would billing you for my services. We'll need to commit to at least ninety days to give the ads time to produce, but if you're willing to invest some money in advertising, I'll invest my time in giving you a great campaign, and we'll split the outcome. You'll keep 95 percent, and you'll pay us 5 percent."

With a split the outcome mindset, both parties align to lower expenses and increase profitability and effectiveness. That means this collaboration will cost the artist less on his advertising as he takes advantage of the volume discounts available to the marketer, plus he'll have professionals to give him a marketing edge, allowing him to focus on his Vision and Capabilities. The marketer doesn't have any expenses other than time and can make money doing what she does best. She doesn't have to worry about getting new one-time clients because she has created a recurring income. And with each similar collaboration she adds, she creates value and visibility for her company. The increase in revenue for both will be amazing.

And it's important to note—the marketing professional didn't show up to the procurement office to ask the artist to buy her services. She showed up at the receiving dock with a Vision of the future and how to help create a future where they split the outcome. This strategy will help the marketing professional grow significantly faster than others with marketing capabilities. Stop right now and think about how you can leverage what you've learned so far. Where can you start at the receiving dock instead of the procurement office with your services?

The Legal Stuff

For those who get hung up on the legal stuff, you'll be relieved to know my team has drawn up a Declaration of Collaboration for members of our CoLAB community who want to collaborate. The declaration lays out the basic and most essential aspects and provides clarity for everyone involved. It includes:

1. What will we call the collaboration?

2. Who does the collaboration involve?

3. Who will we serve? Who is our Hero Target?

4. How are we creating value? What does each person or entity bring to the table?

5. How will we split the outcome?

Check out the declared collaborations from CoLAB Partners in the CoLABhub. Scan the QR code to sign up today.

To ensure the success of your collaboration, I recommend you enlist the help of a neutral party, a Switzerland. Let's face it, we are all human; disputes will arise. In my research of partnerships, I discovered most could have survived if they had a third party divest of interest in either side.

SEEDSPARK's CoLAB provides a facilitator, a third party that becomes Switzerland. We call them CoLAB Architects. These men and women are seasoned entrepreneurs who have two to ten businesses of their own and have studied the art of collaboration and are further along in their activation of their CQ. As CoLAB Partners, they execute the CoLAB-OS for each collaboration they are assigned, and they are compensated for their service out of the Collaboration Currency of one percent that CoLAB receives. They meet monthly or quarterly via Zoom® to evaluate the success and the needs of the collaboration and to make sure that everyone only contributes what comes naturally to them. More importantly, they help identify new collaborations for the CoLAB Partners.

These collaborations often grow quickly, making it easy for new partners to slide back into a competition mindset. They'll think they need to hire more or increase their risk. The CoLAB Architect ensures the partners don't forget how they achieved such growth. When growth causes friction, it's an invitation for a new collaboration. The Architect's only bias is ensuring the collaboration works smoothly and continues to leverage the power of collaboration to grow like no one else.

The Unconventional Key

By now, you can sense a massive departure from the way you've always done things. Maybe you think it's too simple, but I find the most simple things have the most profound impact. Are you beginning to find it difficult to argue with the opportunity and reward this code creates with significantly less time and effort? You've probably even thought of a couple of collaborations you've witnessed but didn't understand the phenomenal growth—until now. Now you know those entrepreneurs were leveraging the VCR formula and the power of collaboration.

Sure, you can keep handing out proposals, signing contracts, and stifling your employees' ideas. After all, everybody does it that way, but if everyone else jumped off a bridge.... Or you can give up on those time-consuming conventions like the linear methods of applying more people, more leases, more inventory, more warehouses, more trucks, more effort, and collaborate.

Today is the day to decide to abandon convention and competition and see the opportunities and resources the world offers those who show up looking for the emergent that arises when you combine. You may be amazed to discover many others in the world who have also started their collaboration journey—men and women tired of the hamster wheel, ready to find someone whose ideas and passions align with theirs, people who want to combine VCRs to create something new and valuable, entrepreneurs who know they are destined for more.

Chapter Seven

Collaborations

Over the years, I've noticed that most entrepreneurs are exhausted. The traditional model of growth creates burnout and bottlenecks. When you look at those percentages I shared in Chapter Six, I see many entrepreneurs carrying enormous risk as they attempt to build full businesses. They spend 80 to 90 percent of their time, energy, and money learning HR techniques, managing operations, and coordinating logistics. But their goal is monetizing their Vision, AKA their unique value contribution. If they could, they'd dedicate 100 percent of their time to this part of their budget, and it's the part responsible for only 10 to 20 percent of the expenses. Entrepreneurs don't need more grind; they need a way to get off the hamster wheel and combine better.

Now that you've started to remove your conventional lenses and exchanged them for growth glasses, you are beginning to see clearly the value of the Code to Collaboration. Your mindset has started to shift from competition to combination. You've inventoried some of your VCR assets and started banking your Collaboration Currency. You understand the value of C3—Collect, Combine, and Create—and your RAKE, which continually expands your VCR Portfolio. I'm also confident you started remembering those objectives and ideas you didn't know how to take action on before. But now, everything's changed.

I love theories and concepts, but I'm not big on small talk. I was built for achievement. It's at the top of my CliftonStrengths®, and my 3-1 PRINT® assessment reveals my need to achieve and succeed and ensure things are perfect, right, and correct. The practical application of collaboration is inspiring.

I've had people ask, "What type of businesses benefit from collaboration?"

I answer, "Every type."

But it's not just for businesses. Activating this new mindset can benefit students, leaders, organizations, and countries. And bringing people ready to collaborate together is what we do at CoLAB.

When I met Stelios, I had already been on a twenty-five-year journey creating businesses from friction identification, experiencing unconventional results in almost every industry. I felt confident in my VCR assets, and I always had a knack for naming things; however, I didn't know the depth of why.

Horizontal growth worked well in my early years. As the owner of an agriculture store, I added more and more products. Later, I added company after company. I operated on a linear-focused growth model with non-linear tactics. I dabbled in collaboration, but didn't fully understand it.

Then, I attended my first Strategic Coach Free Zone Frontier® workshop with Dan Sullivan. I remember it like it was yesterday. I sat there in my own head and started running scenarios for combining one of my company's Capabilities with a client's Reach to create value for those we both served. When Dan began to share his vision for Free Zone collaborations, I started to feel strange inside. It was as if he was describing what I saw in my head. Suddenly, I wasn't alone in the way I saw an opportunity for everyone to grow faster. My unconventional combining had always made me feel out of place, but now I could see the entire matrix of how.

As Dan talked, I wrote. "Next Business—built on collaboration to work with entrepreneurs to leverage the power of collaboration and make it global." Until that moment, I hadn't narrowed my focus to my unique platform.

Though I saw things unconventionally, I still followed many best practices. I could see a better way, I just couldn't articulate or systematize what I did. I thought everyone did it the same. I'd forgotten those words from my childhood: you are special, unique, one of a kind. You too?

CoLAB

That has all changed. When I returned to Charlotte, I couldn't shake what I'd written. I started looking at everything through a different lens, allowing my unconventional thinking to refine my secret sauce and build that global entrepreneurial community I saw when Dan spoke.

The CoLAB community is where I now wield my highest unique value contribution. Collaboration is the absolute unlock, and as Strategic Coach helped me discover, uncovering opportunities that deliver exponential impact by connecting dots in unconventional ways is my Unique Ability.

I found only one thing missing, and it goes back to the problem we had as children. Every group and assessment helped me recognize my uniqueness, but no one told me how to apply what I learned. That's why I started CoLAB. I knew I had to share the Code to Collaboration.

If you looked at the number of companies I started before I envisioned CoLAB, you might guess I have always had more ideas than I had time or resources to carry them out. But the more I got in touch with my full identity and purpose, the more I looked around and saw others with a similar problem—more ideas than avenues to accomplish them. I realized most people have a *WHO* (With the Help of Others) *Deficiency*™.

Many entrepreneurs look for ways to accomplish tasks. But as Dan Sullivan suggests in his book *Who Not How*®, collaboration invites us to look for a Who instead. Exponential growth isn't created by doing more. It's created by combining more.

Now I'm on a journey to turn my purpose into a platform that will give others a place to leap into their whole identity. While I call CoLAB a community—and it is—I envision it becoming a global movement. CoLAB is becoming a place where collaboration becomes culture. Vision is transformed into possibility, Capability turns into shared strength, and Reach becomes exponential amplification.

I love helping entrepreneurs activate their Collaborative Intelligence and unlock their Freedom of Vision through collaborations. Nothing gives me more energy than working with a high-performing entrepreneur or corporate executive to help them identify VCR assets they had no idea existed and empower them as they learn to use their RAKE. However, I can only help those who are ready to crack the code to become Exponential Entrepreneurs. Taking advantage of all you have already been given demands a mindset shift, a journey, and support. It's easy to fall back on the wiring the last twenty-five to forty years of your life has installed.

Decoding Collaborative Intelligence unleashes unimaginable power that allows you to grow like you've never grown before.

We built The CoLAB ecosystem purposefully. I continue to do exactly what I am built for—identifying friction, seeing patterns, and creating, through the art of collaboration, a unique value service or product where everyone wins. Each component of the ecosystem, the CoLAB Community, CoLABhub, CoLAB Exchange, and CoLABra, along with CoLAB Architects, the Declaration of Collaboration, and other CoLAB Resources, solves for friction and powers CQ.

CoLABra allows CoLAB Partners to scale. After I recognized that I am the bottleneck, we created this on-demand system to help members identify their VCR assets, manage their Portfolio, and, unlike anything else on the planet, activate them. CoLABra makes the phone ring. You talk to collaborators who can bring your ideas to reality. Imagine waking up each week with a new set of collaboration opportunities curated for you based upon exactly who you are and what you have to give to create value with your ever-expanding VCR.

A Community

The CoLAB community has the wildest array of Collaboration Currency ever gathered in one room. That's why so many have become a part of CoLAB. Some can't even tell you why they initially joined, but they sense they need to be part of it. They want to engage with the hundreds of collaborations born each year.

Few people, even billion-dollar entrepreneurs, truly understand this kind of powerful collaboration. Most haven't defined their VCR. Though they're incredibly successful, they don't recognize the uniqueness of their secret sauce. They know the work they do energizes them, but they haven't begun to collaborate with themselves. CoLAB helps with that. And if they get stuck, CoVision, CoLAB's collaboration with Stel's brand, Dr. Nik, walks them past the obstacle and breaks the chains that hold them back.

We've developed a culture of giving what you've been given, which empowers members to turn their purpose into a platform. The mindset shift means you don't operate the same. The name on your door may say pest control, professor, mechanic, or student, but the way you do what you do is unlike anyone with the same job description on the door. Recognizing that, I developed CoLAB to turn your secret sauce into your next business. Here, you are not alone. In this community, you can dream bigger.

Whether you're an independent orthopedic surgeon, bricklayer, software developer, broker, or middle school teacher, the way you do what you do is the place I want to help you shift your focus. It's why people do business with you, and the reason you received a thank-you note months after you finished the project.

CoLAB was created to find the extra performance that lies within every person. Our three-step process makes each "I Am" bigger than anyone previously imagined. We Identify, Align, and Multiply (I AM)—by *Identifying* the assets of CoLAB members and *Aligning* the entrepreneurs and creatives who have complementary VCRs. When these two or three collaborators bring their specialties together, *Multiplication* explodes!

Although collaborations at CoLAB begin with business leaders and high-level creatives, the culture can easily permeate every aspect of life. When CoLAB members grasp the power and authenticity of collaboration, they bring this mindset back to their teams and implement it within their organizations. Do you remember Shirley and Joey? Because an Exponential Entrepreneur began to see the power of collaboration within the team, great things happened. But it goes even further.

The real magic happens when Shirley starts the conversation at the dinner table about what they're going to do with her share of the collaboration's profits. A trip to Disney® means the power of collaboration impacts Shirley's children, and they start asking questions.

Suddenly, a new generation becomes interested and educated on the potential of collaboration and how they can activate their uniqueness in the world.

When civilization turns conversations about collaboration into a culture of collaboration, we will see an explosion of exponential growth.

To alleviate the bottleneck, we've developed a platform, the CoLABhub, that will assist you with your Collaborative Intelligence. This component in the CoLAB ecosystem inventories assets—visions you've been giving away for free, underutilized capabilities, and trusted relationships you haven't considered—and makes matches.

A New Way Forward

I don't understand why we look at the world as a race. Each person has been given tools and wisdom to work together to create value and beauty. Yet, even after we've witnessed how competition destroys, people keep competing.

A collaboration mindset also means a change in the way we view outcomes. When I envision the outcome of worldwide collaborations, I see the impact it can have on humanity. A culture of collaboration reaches much deeper. It appreciates every person's uniqueness and looks for ways to highlight skillsets that the competition mindset dismisses.

The go-givers I work with see more than dollar signs when they collaborate. They envision changed lives and ways to make the world a better place. Revenue is a bonus.

The CoLAB community already includes people from every industry and nearly every continent. This allows us to let our imaginations run wild. Every day, our global WHO Finder expands. As entrepreneurs join the community, they add their Vision, Capabilities, and Reach to CoLABhub and it becomes part of the richness of the group.

Then, the CoLAB Exchange, driven by CoLABra, the CoLAB's AI, matches those ideas to make something better with someone else in the community. Every idea, each friction your business feels becomes a signal sent throughout the community. Suddenly, something you have no clue about shows up in your Exchange feed the next day. Never before have entrepreneurs had such an advantage. Now you have access to the person who holds the passion for exactly what you or your business needs to have explosive growth.

I believe that's why we were put here in the first place. You and I were each created with unique ideas, talents, communities, personalities, and interests, and the ways we can combine them number the same as the stars in the sky or the snowflakes each winter. More than that, those combinations will prove to be every bit as original and magical as the stars and the snow.

Real Life Collaborations

The CoLAB Community has generated hundreds of collaborations. Each one is different in structure, but consistent in pattern. They are a signal: When you see friction differently, you see opportunity differently. The solution often already exists—just not inside your business. So let these examples start to train your eye on what is possible when Vision combines with Capabilities and multiplies with Reach.

TellPay: From Friction to Advantage

Joshua Langemann of Can/Am Technologies and his team experienced various problems with his third party payment processors. The unreasonable lead times and unreliable technology added to the fees and lack of customer support made the whole situation unbearable. He also realized that these companies were making a lot of money through the points of sale his software facilitated, sometimes more than the software was worth. Joshua wasn't trying to solve payment processing. But it was in the way of his clients' journey. He saw it as an opportunity.

Through CoLAB and the collaborative relationships it fosters, Joshua explored a different approach. Instead of paying for a service, Can/Am collaborated with Fiserv and split the outcome. Fiserv's strong compliance, processing, settlement, and banking Capabilities, combined with Can/Am's Reach, allowed them to step into a whole new arena without starting from scratch. A collaboration means both parties become engaged in winning deals. They call the collaboration "Teller Payments." Joshua has more confidence and is able to be far less involved with greater results. Two companies took what they do best and combined them to provide better service and grab a bigger outcome.

Joshua followed the pattern: If friction sits in your client's path, follow it. That's where collaboration lives. The result? Thirty-day-faster implementations, stronger client experience, and a new competitive advantage.

The AI Simplifier: From Overwhelm to Momentum

AI created noise, not clarity. Entrepreneurs froze. Tom Lambotte saw the need for simplicity. Steve French saw the scale. Simplifier meets Multiplier. They combined—fast. Within a week: first cohort. No build. No delay. Batteries included. Entrepreneurs moved again. Pattern: When clarity meets scale, speed follows.

Steve French and his friend Tom Lambotte, a retired AI coach, watched as entrepreneurs started drowning in AI. New models entering the market faster than anyone could imagine were killing their focus, creating noise rather than clarity. Tom saw how stuck these entrepreneurs were becoming, and he had the answer. Steve told me that Tom is what Dan Sullivan calls a Simplifier. He quickly sees the solution to problems. Steve, on the other hand, is a Multiplier. He saw how Tom's solution could be bigger than even Tom pictured. Within one week, Tom went from "I might come out of retirement" to "we're selling our first cohort." Within a few months, high-level entrepreneurs were signing up to learn how to leverage AI. Clarity met scale, and speed followed.

Steve and Tom want entrepreneurs to stop trying to do everything themselves. Steve says that he could have created an AI education business, and Tom could have come out of retirement to run small cohorts on the subject, but neither would have people talking about how the classes changed everything and helped launch passion projects. The two didn't do more; they simply leveraged their strengths and built something that neither could have done alone. Tom had the methodology, and Steve had the ability to multiply it, but they credit CoLAB with giving them a framework for ways to deal with issues, concerns, or problems. With a CoLAB Architect, they had structure. They didn't have to figure out how to navigate the collaboration from scratch. Steve said, "This is what separates this from every other partnership I've been in. The CoLAB framework gave us the confidence to go all in." Best of all, stuck entrepreneurs started moving. The AI Simplifier helped them see increased revenue and view AI as their thinking partner instead of a threat. You can check them out at AI-Simplifier.com.

Steve didn't stop after one win. He repeated the pattern. He saw a new problem: entrepreneurs had ideas but no way to extract or structure them. So he made the same move to combine his expertise with that of others to find a solution. The result was the IP Simplifier. Again, Steve moved with a speed that proves that collaboration isn't a one-time event. It's a system that you can implement over and over.

CombineIQ: From Outsourced Friction to Shared Outcomes

When I asked Kristen McGarr of Adroit Insights (AdroitInsights.com) about the friction she experienced that led to collaboration, she said she had a self-limiting belief regarding scaling. She didn't lack capability; she carried too much of it. Traditional structures made her responsible for outcomes without shared ownership. The default solution would be to hire more, but that solved the wrong problem. CoLAB conversations helped shift her mindset from what she lacked to carry out her idea to an entirely new vision. Our discussions made her start to see the value in her vision. Throwing away the traditional way of thinking about partnership, investments, and vendor relationships meant she no longer had to rely on the limitations of a small team, and let her team build something that never existed before.

The CoLAB Community introduced her to Andrew James of Cerebro Analytics (CerebroAnalytics.com). An early adopter of AI, Andrew built a platform that empowers entrepreneurs to have their previously scattered data from every department work together. He has engineered a gateway to collaboration between all your business systems.

Kristen, whose company develops powerful CRMs, and Andrew have come together to bring the force of his collaborative AI software to CRM systems, installations, and consulting. The result is an intelligent system that reduces sales friction and expands value. The pattern to learn from

Kristen is that if you keep hiring for the same gap, it's not a people problem—it's a structure problem.

Instant IP: From Exposure to Ownership

Kary Oberbrunner, CEO of Igniting Souls and Instant IP[IP], realized that many of his clients had created valuable intellectual property that had never been protected, leaving them exposed and vulnerable. This idea birthed the vision behind Instant IP. It could protect Igniting Souls authors while they were writing their books. But Kary didn't build internally; he collaborated. He engaged Evan Ryan at Teammate AI () to build the technology and IP lawyers to patent the process. Igniting Souls had a new capability that became incredibly valuable through collaboration. Kary pointed out the value of check-ins to ensure progress and collaboration integrity, as well as the need for clarity around your Collaboration Currency. He said that we can create more impact by leveraging our Collaboration Currency. The pattern that Kary's story demonstrates is that when value isn't captured, collaboration turns it into an asset.

Igniting Souls also publishes books like this one. They have the Capability. CoLAB facilitates collaborations, so we have relationships with entrepreneurs. Many CoLAB members would like to write a book; they have a vision. So, CoLAB and Igniting Souls have collaborated. The folks at Igniting Souls will just keep doing what they do well, and CoLAB will continue to facilitate collaborations. When they come together, books get published under the CoVerse imprint, and we split the outcome.

My web design company has also collaborated with that book publisher. In this case, the designer has the Capability, and the publisher has the Reach—many authors who need a website.

Further Collaborations

Dr. Stel Nikolakakis works with some of the world's top entrepreneurs to unblock the things that limit their belief in themselves. When I identify what's holding an entrepreneur back, I leverage Dr. Nik to help release it, unlocking faster, non-linear growth. His work delivers immediate value to CoLAB by freeing entrepreneurs from what's holding them back and unblocking their entrepreneurial vision.

He says that the most beautiful thing about combining is that in collaboration, everyone has skin in the game. Unlike conventional business, where incentives can be misaligned, shared outcomes shape behavior. When everyone knows their role and acts in it, velocity increases and the path to success shortens. Stel feels he's found a fast pass to growth and value creation, and through collaboration, he's been able to create something he never had the resources for before.

After Tony D'Angelo learned about the VCR Formula and combined it with Strategic Coach's Simplifier/Multiplier Collaboration, he realized he had Vision and Capability but lacked the Reach to provide value to a new hero target. One option was to spend time, effort, attention, money, and the skill of his team to create a new platform. But he knew the better plan would be to find a fellow entrepreneur who could bring their multiplier capability of digital delivery to combine with his ability to simplify IP education. Now, Tony and Steve, under the collaboration named IP Simplifier, are empowering growth-minded, ambitious, collaborative entrepreneurs to get their IP out of their heads and on the balance sheet of their IP holding companies so they can license their God-given intellectual property.

When a ghostwriter who specializes in memoirs came to our group, we named his specialty, and he collaborated with several high-end entrepreneurs who have hero targets who will benefit from a memoir—people who are also the ghostwriter's hero targets. Now, his collaboration, which he calls Legacy by Levin, has expanded his Reach, and those in the circle get to introduce their clients to a high-end writer and split the outcome.

Collaborations also mean you don't have to ask for referrals anymore. When you empower someone to elevate their status in the herd, referrals become organic. For instance, if a tax preparer tells me that anyone I send her way will automatically be pushed to the front of the line, she has elevated my status. When I share her information with one of my associates who needs taxes done quickly, I have better standing. I'm naturally going to tell everyone I know who needs the tax preparer's services.

In my world, when I have a Vision, I can either hire people to carry it out, or I can find an entrepreneur who already has a team of people with the capabilities needed to do what I need done. Then we can collaborate and split the outcome. I now understand that collaboration is the key to greater impact, influence, and income.

CoLAB Apprentice™

The world doesn't need more workers. It needs creators, collaborators, and exponential thinkers. That's why we opened a special section of CoLAB for sixteen- to twenty-four-year-old innovators and problem solvers. I get truly excited thinking about helping the next generation and creating a place where they learn to think exponentially, create exponentially, and collaborate exponentially. It's important for young people to be prepared for the Collaboration Economy, so they can step into who they were designed to become.

Teens in CoLAB work with a personal mentor to learn the core elements of CoLAB, including the Just Add a Zero, Remove the Film, and Vision Bank frameworks, as well as each of the concepts you've read about here. They participate in WHO Partnering Practice and Vision Workshops, as well as VCR Mapping for Youth, where they'll identify their unique Vision, Capability, and Reach at an early age.

CoLAB Apprentice also connects aspiring entrepreneurs to CoLAB Partners to leverage VCR and unlock the young person's Collaborative Intelligence. We dedicate ten percent of CoLAB profits to provide scholarships so any young person can learn how to generate ideas effortlessly, collaborate confidently, and turn friction into opportunity.

I want to open the eyes of these high school and college-aged youth to the possibilities and help them build their portfolio of VCR assets. If you know a teen who wants to make an impact and is bored by conventional learning, encourage them to apply. They'll receive mentorship and the tools necessary to shift their mindset from competition to collaboration. By the time they finish the apprenticeship program, they'll be able to leverage collaboration and hopefully become one of our CoLAB partners who look for collaborations.

CoLABhub

Would you like to get a taste of CoLAB? CoLABhub is where you step directly into the experience. It's an open environment designed for real-time collaboration and practical application.

Inside the app, you can explore Collaborative Intelligence and the core concepts of the Code to Collaboration, then put them into action. You'll start by identifying your Vision assets, Capability assets, and Reach assets while exchanging collaboration signals with others doing the same. From there, you learn how to collect, combine, and create.

CoLABhub is a live, ongoing immersion into CoLAB. Use the QR code to access the app and step in.

CoLAB offers unlimited opportunities to share with others who bring their Collaboration Currency to the table. It's the place where Freedom of Vision thrives.

If you're ready to home in on your true identity as an Exponential Entrepreneur, leveraging your VCR by igniting the engine of your Collaborative Intelligence, today's your day. You are unique, special, and gifted like no one else on this planet, and now you know how to activate that knowledge. You have the keys: the Code to Collaboration is the secret to your Freedom of Vision as you move into Desirement.

Chapter Eight

Final Thoughts

I magine the world as millions of Venn Diagrams. Some have two circles, some have four. Others have six circles, and many of the Venn Diagrams overlap each other. In each circle, you find a name with that person's Collaboration Currency, but where the circles overlap, the possibilities are endless. That's the place of Combine in the Creation Code.

The circles' convergence is also my secret sauce. The greatest asset in my Collaboration Currency wallet is Vision. I look at the Venn Diagrams of life and see the emergent. You see, when you combine two things, there's always something emergent. When you and I combine, we create something new and unique, but it's bigger than that. Our collaboration means you are not the same, and I am not the same.

How I See

People used to ask me, "How do you see those collaborations?" And for a time, I couldn't describe it. It's the way I was created. I've been doing it since I was eight. However, I spent much of my time collaborating with myself or creating collaborations with things. I naturally Collected and Combined, and Creations just occurred. For years, every time I ran into friction, I created a business to take care of it or expanded a business I'd already built. I created a great deal of vertical growth.

After digging deep into the steps, my brain processes quickly, and I realized the real power in the Code to Collaboration was horizontal growth—combining with those who had Collaboration Currency I couldn't find in my wallet.

I also realized the world of collaboration is wide open to anyone willing to do these five things:

- Be attentive

- Give up competition

- Learn to collaborate with themselves

- Use the Creation Code

- Uncover their VCR

Anyone willing to do that work can become a creator. And when I meet people implementing those creator steps, I can't help but see collaboration. Something inside me starts to hit rewind and fast-forward when I hear your story and feel your passion. I can envision the experiences in your past that brought you to this moment, and I can see you ten years from now if you follow those passions.

CoLAB Is Really for Me

My passion to help you see the next scene in your movie is why CoLAB exists. I call it my Massively Transformative Project (MTP). Yes, it's a community built to help leaders who want to be creators, but it's also for me. I want to weave collaboration back into the culture of humanity and return us to our original building blocks. The CoLAB community gives me an opportunity to live out my passion to connect the unconventional dots and create exponential impact.

Truthfully, when I share those connections, I don't feel like I'm uncovering anything. Every piece of the puzzle is already lying on the table; I just happen to be the one who can easily see where it fits.

I see with what I call Dimensional Vision Awareness. According to the theory of quantum physics, all possible outcomes exist at the same time. Imagine five people all gazing out over a beautiful field. On one side is a herd of cattle, and on the other side, I see a flock of sheep. Fenced off in the center, some lovely clover grows. However, because we aren't all standing in the same location, I'm the only one who can see the entire field. One person sees the cows, another sees the lambs, and a third doesn't realize anything is in the field because from his vantage point, trees hide everything except the hills in the distance. Though the cattle, sheep, and clover all exist, each person can only see from their perspective.

Everything is possible in the "field," whether you can see it or not. Dimensional Vision Awareness allows me to see the possibilities of every connection in the field like a movie. Not only can I see it from every angle, but I can also see how the field began and where it will be in the future.

Fast-forwarding through the quantum field allows me to see the emergent. My brain envisions the potential outcome, and then my natural curiosity invites me to find the steps that birthed that outcome. I don't create anything; I simply see what already exists, but because of my unusual vantage point, I see things others don't.

You Are the Screenwriter

I often wonder how many people could develop Dimensional Vision Awareness if they cracked the Code to Collaboration and walked into the field of possibilities. I thoroughly enjoy helping people see their movies, but I'm convinced I'm not the only person with that superpower.

For many, the fast-forward button doesn't work because they haven't learned to collaborate with themselves. When we see through the eyes of competition, it blocks our view of the future. Others get so busy watching the reruns in black and white that they don't try to see the past in full color to embrace the way those experiences shaped them. Whether good or bad, everything we enjoyed or endured frames our perspective. They gave us Knowledge and Awareness. Each one added to our individuality. RAKE gives you a framework and a lens to look at the past with perspective.

Sadly, those who get stuck in what was and view it as a black-and-white hindrance rather than mottled clay that can be formed into something beautiful miss the 4D full-color version of their future.

In order to see what's ahead, we have to be totally present in the here and now. We need to know and embrace our superpower and allow everything we do to stream from it. The key is learning to appreciate everything our RAKE has collected.

Every Relationship, Awareness, tidbit of Knowledge, and Experience creates an opportunity to write a new scene in your movie. And that's the most beautiful thing about the Code to Collaboration. It gives you the ability to choose Act II and Act III. Every time we watch the fast-forward, because we've collected more with our RAKE, the ending changes just a bit. We can fast-forward and rewind as many times as necessary until the vision we see for the future speaks to our heart and feeds our passion.

Collaboration invites you to insert who you know, what you know, and where you go into your movie. Everything you need to become a creator already exists. The Code to Collaboration simply gives you the keys to see the emergent. This is where the magic happens.

The Intentionality of Collaboration

When we're honest with ourselves, we realize nothing happens without collaboration. I've never done anything by myself. Without collaboration, I would just exist in the ether. The second I gain consciousness every morning, I begin to collaborate.

I collaborate with the air as it enters my lungs and the sounds of my house as they fill my ears. My gratitude allows me to collaborate with the Creator, and my gym time lets my body collaborate with itself as the parts work together to stay healthy.

Cracking the Code to Collaboration means you have embraced some undeniable truths:

- You have been built with a unique superpower.

- You can only give what you've been given, but you already have everything you need to create.

- You have a Vision—an idea for improvement.

- You have Capabilities, and you use them in a way no one else can.

- You have Reach, people who trust you and love the way you use your superpower.

- You are an entrepreneur, a creator who can take things to the next level.

There you have it—the Creation Code and the Code to Collaboration. When you take those keys and combine them with everything you've already been given, you start to see the magic. Only one thing is left to make you unstoppable—becoming deliberate. Intentionality puts you in the right mindset, but acting deliberately is the key to the inner sanctum of collaboration.

In the inner sanctum, every moment has purpose—including the days I rest. Strategic Coach calls them Free Days®. Yes, deliberately taking action for self-care sits at the top of the list for the highest performers.

Intense intentionality as you Collect and Combine and inventory your RAKE and VCR will expand your vision to 5D. Everything in the fast-forward of your movie becomes so clear it collapses into the current reality, allowing you to add deliberate and calculated action to bring your intentions into reality.

The Definition of an Entrepreneur

At the very beginning, I shared the definition of an entrepreneur: someone who shifts economic resources out of an area of lower and into an area of higher productivity and greater yield. But one of the things I've witnessed to be common in true entrepreneurs is the passion to relentlessly seek leverage. They leverage the resources within their grasp and take them from one performance level to a higher performance level.

And the only way you're able to do that is to recombine what already exists. That's what gives you leverage: the ability to combine, to create, to collaborate.

If you call yourself an entrepreneur, but you aren't leveraging collaboration, I want to challenge you to reconsider your title. Are you truly an entrepreneur, or are you simply a business owner?

There's nothing wrong with being a business owner. The world has hundreds of companies that need someone to own and run them.

On the other hand, if you like the idea of being an entrepreneur, you need to look at the places where you are relentlessly seeking to leverage the resources you've been given.

All the resources in the world already exist. There's nothing new, only new combinations. Take a minute to review your last three years. What have you combined during that time? Have you added new people to your team? Did you combine with a new location?

If you want to carry the title of entrepreneur, it's time to deliberately, passionately, and relentlessly Combine and Create from the things you Collect in your RAKE to leverage collaboration.

You Possess the Code

How disappointed would you have been if your favorite hero or heroine had abandoned the treasure after finding the code? *Indiana Jones, The Da Vinci Code, Enigma*, and *The Imitation Game* all would have left us baffled if they hadn't found the treasure or completed the task.

You now possess the key that will allow you to be someone's hero.

This planet needs your Vision. Without it, there will always be a piece missing from the grand portrait. You have been given great gifts, and now you know the path that leads to bringing that Vision to life and giving back what you've been given.

But will you join me on the journey? Will you add your piece to the puzzle?

Don't say someday or put this book on a shelf and your Vision on a to-do list. Take the keys you've been handed and open the lock. Now is the time to embrace your uniqueness, unleash your superpower, and share it with the world.

As you have read this book, I hope your true potential has begun to shine through. I'm confident you have ideas brewing. Everyone does. I want this book to help you recognize them and help you see that collaboration provides the natural way to move them from ideas to vision to reality.

When I started writing, I was driven by what I see, and what I see missing. I see a world full of genius just waiting to be combined to create. I see a multitude of ideas stuck on the shelf of your imagination warehouse, ready for you to bring them out and create change in the world.

I chose a puzzle with the missing piece just waiting to be added as the cover of this book. I want that picture to stay in your head to remind you of two intrinsic truths. One: You are the missing piece of the puzzle. The world needs every bit of you—your uniqueness, your ideas, your experiences—everything that makes you who you are. The puzzle isn't complete until the real you shows up. Number two: I want it to remind you of the missing piece to your personal puzzle. You don't have to do this alone. It's time to recognize your WHO Deficiency and recognize that you'll find the missing piece in collaboration. It's that simple.

As a society, it's time to turn our sights toward putting the pieces in place. Let's start having fun and play matchmaker with the immense number of Unique Value Contributions you can find around the world.

I am on a mission to unlock the power of humanity by restoring the art of collaboration to our culture. Thank you for taking the time to read this book and for your consideration to start leveraging collaboration to be all you can be through Collecting, Combining, and Creating.

Appendix: The Collaboration Code in Practice

This appendix exists for one reason: application.

The chapters of *The Code to Collaboration* are designed to expand your vision and specifically how you see yourself, others, and what's possible when people combine intentionally. What follows is optional, practical material to help you translate insight into action.

You do not need to read this appendix to understand the book. You may want it if you're ready to implement what you've discovered.

Appendix A: The VCR Framework (Vision, Capability, Reach)

At the heart of collaboration is a simple truth: No one has everything, but everyone has something. The VCR framework is a way to inventory what you bring into collaboration and identify what's missing.

- Vision – The ability to see what could exist before it does.

- Capability – The skills, systems, or processes that make something real.

- Reach – Access to people, trust, distribution, or demand.

Every successful collaboration contains all three—rarely in one person.

Use this framework to:

- Clarify your unique value contribution.

- Spot collaboration gaps quickly.

- Replace "Who should I hire?" with "Who should I collaborate with?"

Expand your understanding of VCR by reading *The VCR Formula* by Dean Jackson and Chad T. Jenkins. Plus, watch for the next book in the VCR series that Dean and Chad plan to introduce at each CoLABcon.

Appendix B: Types of Collaboration

Not all collaborations are the same. Understanding the type clarifies expectations, outcomes, and structure.

The four foundational collaboration types explored in this work include:

- Partner Collaborations

- Referral Collaborations

- Joint Venture Collaborations

- Growth Collaborations

Each type serves a different purpose, but all are built on shared value creation and aligned hero targets.

Appendix C: Naming and Declaring Collaborations

Collaborations become real when they are named. A named collaboration:

- Creates clarity

- Builds commitment

- Establishes shared ownership

- Signals seriousness to everyone involved

The practice of naming and declaring collaborations transforms loose ideas into intentional outcomes. This is where imagination becomes operational.

Download our tool (Name the Baby™) to help you name your collaboration here: SEEDSPARK.com/tools

Appendix D: A Simple Collaboration Inventory Exercise

Ask yourself:

1. What Vision do I hold that others don't?

2. What Capabilities do I consistently use to create value?

3. Where do I already have Reach, trust, or access?

4. Where am I trying to do alone what could be combined?

5. Who comes to mind immediately as a natural collaborator?

Your answers are not static. They evolve as you collaborate. So be sure to come back to this exercise at least annually.

Appendix E: Desirement

The next book on my agenda will expand the idea of desirement. I want to help you understand the flywheel in more detail and set people free from working toward retirement to living with a career in desirement. If you'd like to be on the list to be notified when it's ready and get one of the one hundred signed copies I'm going to give away, scan the QR code at the right.

A Final Note on the Appendix

This appendix is not a checklist to complete—it's a resource to return to.

True collaboration is not something you finish. It's something you practice.

As your awareness expands, so will the opportunities to connect, combine, and create value far beyond what you could accomplish alone.

Endnotes

1. *The Economist.* "Entrepreneurship." April 27, 2009.
   https://www.economist.com/news/2009/04/27/entrepreneurship.

2. Dawe GS, Tan XW, Xiao ZC. "Cell migration from baby to mother." *Cell Adh Migr.*
   2007;1(1):19-27.

3. Bob Burg and John David Mann. *The Go-Giver: A Little Story About a Powerful Business
   Idea.* Portfolio, 2007.

4. 60 Minutes. *YouTube.* "Tom Brady on Winning." January 31, 2019.
   https://www.youtube.com/watch?v=-TA4_fVkv3c

5. Clark Joanne. *Destiny Pursuit.* "The Construction of Reality to 2
   Million Bits of Info-NLP Matters, Episode #038." February 11, 2021.
   https://www.destinypursuit.com.au/nlpmatters/038-construction-of-reality

6. Jobs, Steve. "Creativity is just connecting things." qtd. In "Steve Jobs Quotes." *Goodreads.*
   Accessed December 9, 2025.
   https://www.goodreads.com/quotes/1031045-creativity-is-just-connecting-things-when-
   you-ask-creative-people

7. *Statista.* "McDonalds Stats and Figures." May 16, 2025.
   https://www.statista.com/topics/1444/mcdonalds/?srsltid=AfmBOor9IN4rQLIpQmc
   CGCVD5viNV8-t3fxQS2d132NamCXOVX_EM2ry#topicOverview.

8. *StockX.* "Nike Air Force 1 Low." Accessed October 31, 2025.
   https://stockx.com/nike-air-force-1-low-sp-tiffany-and-co.

9. *Formula One.* "Lewis Hamilton." Accessed October 17, 2025.
   https://www.formula1.com/en/drivers/lewis-hamilton.

10. Nicole, Emily. *The Sporting News.* "Lewis Hamilton hopeful of Ferrari turnaround at US
    Grand Prix." October 17, 2025.
    https://www.sportingnews.com/uk/formula-1/news/lewis-hamilton-hopeful-ferrari-tur
    naround-us-grand-prix/.

Acknowledgments

This book exists because collaboration exists.

While my name is on the cover, the thinking, insight, courage, and momentum behind *The Code to Collaboration* came through countless conversations, shared experiments, and moments of collective curiosity.

This work is the result of people willing to combine, not compete.

First, my deepest gratitude goes to my family.

To my wife, Jennifer—thank you for your patience, belief, and unwavering support through 50-plus organizations, and while this idea evolved from intuition to language to platform. Your presence grounded me when my vision ran far ahead of the calendar.

To my daughters, **Adelaide,** whose detailed visions continue to amaze me, and to **Carson**, your relentless intuition of value creation gives even me a run for my money—you both remind me daily why building a better future through collaboration actually matters.

To my CoLAB Partners—thank you for sharpening this work by challenging it, questioning it, and expanding it. You didn't just listen to these ideas—you lived them. You proved, again and again, that when Vision, Capability, and Reach are intentionally combined, time collapses on the road to success.

And finally, to you, **the reader**. By choosing this book, you're already participating in the code. My hope is that what you discover here doesn't give you something new—but helps you unlock what you already have, so you can combine it with others in ways that create exponential value for all. It's all a collaboration.

This book is not mine alone. It never was.

Meet Chad T. Jenkins

Chad T. Jenkins built more than fifty companies by doing one thing differently: turning overlooked friction in outdated, margin-compressed industries into collaborative leverage that reignites profit.

Along the way, he discovered something most entrepreneurs feel but rarely name. Founders often have more opportunities than they can execute, while others have exactly the Vision, Capability, or reach to bring those ideas to life. The problem is nothing connecting them.

That realization changed everything.

Chad defines an entrepreneur as someone who instinctively seeks leverage in all things. Today, he no longer builds companies. He builds collaborations.

Through CoLAB by SEEDSPARK®, entrepreneurs uncover their Collaboration Currency, their unique blend of Vision, Capability, and Reach. Inside CoLABhub with the CoLAB Exchange, they do what comes naturally: connect, combine, and create.

It all started as a belief. Chad was told, like all of us, that he was made unique. What he realized is that uniqueness becomes truly powerful when combined. Through CoLABra, entrepreneurs bring their biggest ideas and are matched with the people and resources to activate them. No need to own everything. No need to build alone.

For over 200 years, that's exactly what entrepreneurs have been told to do. He is changing that.

Before You Join
CoLAB, Experience It.

You already have what you need to create more than you ever wanted. Join the global community of CoLAB Partners, and experience the thinking, tools, and dynamics that make collaboration actually work so you can create tomorrow, together.

Try CoLABhub
For Free Today!

Take the
CQ Assessment
in CoLABhub!

Inside CoLABhub you will uncover your unique blend of Vision, Capability, and Reach with our CQ Assessment. Get matched with aligned collaborators based on your results and start turning connection into exponential growth.

Use Code TENOFFCQ for 10% off the CQ Assessment!

Explore CoVerse™

The Code to Collaboration is part of CoVerse™ – a collection of books exploring Vision, Capability, and Reach in the Collaboration Economy™.

Discover our authors and continue your collaboration journey

View All CoVerse™ Books & Authors